ENDOR

I love Candice Smithyman's passion for the Lord, His Kingdom, and His presence. Her heart is to see believers come into the fullness of all God has for them and to live "on earth as it is in heaven." I have a great love for the subject of this book.

DR. PATRICIA KING
Author, Television Host, Minister
www.patriciaking.com

The Holy Spirit has specific themes He highlights and addresses in different seasons. The Holy Spirit also selects specific messengers to be carriers of that word in those seasons. The subject of Heaven on earth is one of those strategic themes and Candice Smithyman is one of those anointed chosen messengers. Do yourself a favor and get two copies of *Releasing Heaven*, get one for yourself and another as a gift for a friend. Thank you, Candice, for being a faithful, available servant of the Lord.

JAMES W. GOLL
God Encounters Ministries
GOLL Ideation LLC
www.godencounters.com

Get this book *Releasing Heaven* into the earth and into your personal life. Candice Smithyman's words JUMPED off the page to me when she wrote: "Everyone who believes that Jesus Christ is our Lord and Savior is not only born again… You are now considered to be a portal to heaven, you are now a heavenly being in an earthsuit—but more than that, you are eternity in action." You and I are in a time and season on earth where all of Heaven is crying out along with myriads of intercessors on the earth—all to bring Heaven's desires into the earth. God just keeps saying to me, "Study Heaven" and

"Learn more of Heaven's secrets." Have I gotten your attention? Get this book!

STEVE SHULTZ
Founder, The Elijah List & Elijah Streams TV program.
www.elijahlist.com

In *Releasing Heaven,* Dr. Candice Smithyman has written a powerful and riveting book that will help all believers establish their identity for heavenly encounters and teach them about creating a supernatural environment for releasing Heaven on earth. Dr. Candice has done a masterful job as a prophet of God leaving us keys to accessing the heavens similar to our ancient biblical prophets and predecessors. This is a must-read primer loaded with revelatory pearls within each chapter. She shares profound revelation that literally unearths truths hidden in the true identity of the believer in Christ—we carry God's DNA and spiritual genetics that reveal us as portals waiting for Heaven to manifest in and through. You will learn in this book that we have been made the portals of God on earth and that every encounter with the God of Heaven creates an opportunity and environment of *Releasing Heaven!*

DR. NAIM COLLINS
President of Naim Collins Ministries
League of the Prophets
Wilmington, Delaware
Author of *Realms of the Prophetic*
www.naimcollinsministries.com

As you read this book, *Releasing Heaven,* you will have a better understanding of Heaven and you will be put on a collision course to understand who you really are. You are a carrier of God's glory and you too can release Heaven every day, wherever you go! This book is for people who are really looking to understand their identity for eternity. No matter what stage of life you are in, this book will give you tools that will equip you to go higher. Get ready—you are on a collision course to excel. It's a game changer.

ANGELA GREENIG
Angela Greenig Ministries
www.angelagreenig.com

I appreciate the encouragement and inspiration Pastor Candice Smithyman brings through her book, *Releasing Heaven: Creating a Supernatural Environment through Heavenly Encounters.* Learning how to host the presence of God and recognize His ways is extremely important to being able to flow in His power and experience His supernatural presence. These encounters bring amazing changes to our life, resulting in more faith, surrender, power, understanding, and fruit. I appreciate Candice's jealousy for the presence of God that brings revelation of His holiness, majesty, power, and love.

DR. RANDY CLARK
Founder, Global Awakening
www.globalawakening.com

Candice Smithyman writes from her own experience of heavenly encounters and visions and she encourages us that these encounters are not just for her, but for every believer. She gives thought-renewing ideas to change your thinking to walk in and experience the supernatural. I have witnessed the glory of God exuding from Dr. Smithyman; therefore, she is not simply writing about an experience, but continually living it and drawing you into the desire to manifest this same glory in your life.

APOSTLE KATHY DEGRAW
Founder, Kathy DeGraw Ministries
Host, Prophetic Spiritual Warfare Podcast Show
Author of *Discerning and Destroying the Works of Satan* and *Speak Out*
www.kathydegrawministries.org

When I first heard the title for Dr. Candice's new book, I was immediately hooked. *Releasing Heaven: Creating a Supernatural*

Environment through Heavenly Encounters is a "right now" message for the body of Christ. The Church is entering what will be her finest hour. A selfless Bride passionate for the manifest presence of her beloved Bridegroom, and passionate to see the brightness of His glory consume the darkness of this world. Yes. It is time. It is time for the Church to begin walking in the fullness of God's power and glory. If your heart is longing for an authentic expression of Heaven, then get ready, because this book takes you on a journey into the supernatural.

ROD W. LARKINS
Pastor, Deep Water Ministries
Author of *Overflow* and *You Are the Apple of God's Eye*
www.rodwlarkins.com

Candice Smithyman's book *Releasing Heaven* is a beautiful account of her experiences in Heaven and a clarion call to the entire Body of Christ to arise into Heaven and receive the fullness of all God's blessings! Paul told believers to "set their affections on the things above," and this book clearly reveals what he had in mind. I urge you to read, digest, and apply what is in this book. I promise that you can have a supernatural lifestyle too!

JOAN HUNTER
Author, Healing Evangelist
Miracles Happen! TV Show Host
www.joanhunter.org

Candice Smithyman lives her life with positive passion for Jesus. She has found ways of making encountering God easy and practical, yet she is a very deep and gifted teacher and prophetic coach who has a relevant message for the emerging church. Her latest book, *Releasing Heaven: Creating a Supernatural Environment through Heavenly Encounters*, will open the heavens over you to experience the gift of God's joy and love.

DOUG ADDISON
Author of *Hearing God Every Day*, the Daily Prophetic Word, and *The Spirit Connection* Webcast, Podcast, and Blog
www.DougAddison.com

Dr. Candice Smithyman is a mega-Word woman—she knows the Bible and lives it! She responds to God with great obedience and faith and conducts herself with integrity. In the pages of this book you will learn about how to release Heaven into your environments by walking out the faith of God through His Word. As a miracle worker myself, I know the battle and victory associated with operating in healing and miracles—and Dr. Candice shares these challenges and how to overcome them in her book.

KATIE SOUZA
Founder, Katie Souza Ministries
www.Katiesouza.com

It is an honor to enthusiastically endorse Dr. Candice Smithyman's book, *Releasing Heaven: Creating a Supernatural Environment through Heavenly Encounters*. As a prophetic harpist who teaches on the intersection of the spiritual realm and God's quantum universe, I resonate with Dr. Smithyman's approach to imparting to her readers how to create a supernatural environment for heavenly encounters. Her concept of how we can act as people who are "eternity in action" powerfully activates the believer to draw from God's timeless power, NOW! She does not have a "theoretical theology," but provides a practical, life-changing instruction manual on how to change the spiritual atmosphere around you. Dr. Smithyman's life is transparent as she shares her deep, real-life experiences in God, revealing how she came to understand how we can be the very gateway to Heaven.

MICHAEL-DAVID
Psalmist, Inventor
Author of *The Frequency of the Supernatural*
www.michael-david.org

When you said yes to Jesus Christ, you were not only saved and given eternal life, you became the overlap between Heaven and earth. Jesus restored you to relationship with your heavenly Father and all of His Kingdom. Not only so you will go to Heaven one day, but so that you can bring Heaven into the earth every day you are here. Or to put it more simply, you are not "normal." You are a supernatural agent of impact for the Kingdom here in the earth. Dr. Smithyman's new book will help you leave "normal" behind and step into the fullness of what you said yes to when you received Jesus as your Lord and Savior. The Kingdom of Heaven is within you (see Luke 17:21), and it wants out! You are meant to release the reality of Heaven to everyone you meet, everywhere you go, all to the glory of Jesus Christ. *Releasing Heaven* will help you step into that divine mandate and glorious purpose.

ROBERT HOTCHKIN
Minister, Author, Media Host
Men on the Frontlines / Patricia King Ministries
RobertHotchkin.com / Menonthefrontlines.com

In her latest book, *Releasing Heaven,* Pastor Candice Smithyman presents us with a treasure chest of revelation and understanding that will empower our ability to shift spiritual atmospheres and connect the heavenly realms into our earthly dimension. It is full of powerful prophetic insight, amazing scriptural teaching, dynamic word studies and enriching testimonies. A must read for every believer!

Dr. Jane Hamon
Co-Apostle of Vision Church @ Christian International
Author of *Dreams and Visions, The Deborah Company,
The Cyrus Decree,* and *Discernment*

RELEASING
HEAVEN

RELEASING
HEAVEN

Creating a
SUPERNATURAL ENVIRONMENT
through HEAVENLY ENCOUNTERS

CANDICE SMITHYMAN

DESTINY IMAGE® PUBLISHERS, INC.
P.O. Box 310, Shippensburg, PA 17257-0310
"Promoting Inspired Lives."

This book and all other Destiny Image and Destiny Image Fiction books are available at Christian bookstores and distributors worldwide.

Cover design by Eileen Rockwell
Interior design by Terry Clifton

For more information on foreign distributors, call 717-532-3040.
Reach us on the Internet: www.destinyimage.com.

ISBN 13 TP: 978-0-7684-5231-0
ISBN 13 eBook: 978-0-7684-5232-7
ISBN 13 HC: 978-0-7684-5234-1
ISBN 13 LP: 978-0-7684-5233-4

For Worldwide Distribution, Printed in the U.S.A.
1 2 3 4 5 6 7 8 / 24 23 22 21 20

DEDICATION

I dedicate this book to the only One who deserves the glory—my Jesus Christ. Through the heavenly encounters I have had through the Holy Spirit this book is made possible.

I also dedicate this writing to my husband, Adam Smithyman, and our three beautiful children, Alexandria, Nicholas, and Samantha, and their spouses.

Acknowledgments

I thank my husband, Adam, for his patience with my time being consumed to write this book and share the heavenly experience with others. My daughter, Alexandria, who works for Dream Mentors and edits all my television programs and keeps the message of heavenly encounters going out to the world.

Also, to my Freedom Destiny Church family who consistently through worship create an atmosphere where heavenly encounters with God are usual. Pastor Iana Harris and Pastor Dina Duchene who work tirelessly with Freedom Destiny Church and Dream Mentors International to help us teach, train, and transform the lives of those whom God has given us to mentor. Elder Debbi Shon, my close friend and confident who through many years has held my husband, Adam, and I up in prayer and support. I am eternally grateful to the partners and friends of our ministries who give sacrificially in prayer and finances as without them this book and our media outreaches are not possible.

Megan Nikki Prav who gave her time to read and make the first edits for each chapter of this book.

Dr. Hakeem Collins who first pitched this book to Destiny Image Publishers on my behalf and has believed in it ever since he heard the title, *Releasing Heaven*. Tina Pugh, for standing with me and encouraging me to keep pressing and making a way for the revelation in this book to go forth.

I especially want to thank my sister Debra Hodgson for her love and support, and I want to acknowledge the woman who always encourages me and who has had many angelic encounters in her walk with God, my mother, Joan Borland Rainsberger.

CONTENTS

Foreword *by Dr. Hakeem Collins*   1

Introduction   7

PART I   **ESTABLISHING IDENTITY FOR HEAVENLY ENCOUNTERS**   11

Chapter 1   You Are Eternity in Action   13

Chapter 2   You Can Release Heaven   27

Chapter 3   Gateway to Heaven   39

Chapter 4   Open Heaven Manifestations   55

Chapter 5   Heavenly Pillar   73

PART II   **HEAVENLY ENCOUNTERS THAT CREATE SUPERNATURAL ENVIRONMENTS**   87

Chapter 6   Caught Up to Heaven   89

Chapter 7   Heavenly Riches   99

Chapter 8   Accessing Heavenly Treasuries   113

Chapter 9   Releasing Captives Through Heavenly Strategies   131

Chapter 10   You Are Enough   147

Chapter 11   Angel Turnaround   167

Chapter 12   Angel Intervention   181

Chapter 13   The Faith of God for Miracles   197

Chapter 14   Jesus Is Willing to Heal   211

Chapter 15   The Heavenly Courtroom   225

Conclusion   245

FOREWORD

Dr. Hakeem Collins

I was invited on a television digital broadcast for *Spirit Fuel* TV hosted by Dr. Candice Smithyman. While on the show, Dr. Candice and I began to share divine revelation as it pertains to the supernatural, angels, healing, mental freedom, soul wounds, deliverance, and the miraculous power of God through the Holy Spirit. Right there on the broadcast was such a culture of Heaven being imparted, released, and established that viewers were being healed, set free, and touched by the love and power of God.

After the show had ended, I wanted to hear more about what was in her heart and what is God saying in this season for the Body of Christ. Dr. Smithyman started to unravel and unfold an insight that God gave her and that she has been writing, teaching, and imparting this revelation from the Lord in her church, her own television show,

Glory Road TV, and wherever she travels across the country. I personally wanted to know more, being that I am an inquisitive person and love to hear the prophetic Word of God. She called this prophetic insight and divine revelation *Releasing Heaven!*

I was awestruck by the title initially, and when I learned later it was to become a book concept, I was so intrigued that I pitched the idea to my acquisition agent with Destiny Image Publishers. That being said, what you are holding in your hands is the genesis and the first volume of a series of spiritual, divine, prophetic revelation on how to create a culture of Heaven here and now!

My dear friend and sister, Dr. Candice Smithyman, has been called of God with dualistic mandates, prophetically and apostolically, to help Spirit-filled believers create spaces and places of *habitation* of God's presence—more than just spaces and places of *visitation.*

Releasing Heaven is a groundbreaking literary handbook with keys to supernaturally shifting atmospheres and learning how to ascend to the Courts of Heaven to receive favorable verdicts, outcomes, favors, and benefits. Furthermore, while reading this book I believe that the eyes of your heart will be enlightened so that you may know what is the hope to which God has called you and what are the riches of His glorious inheritance in you as a believer. This literary work is infused with heavenly encounters by the Father that will activate the faith within you to reach beyond mediocrity and move into a realm of possibilities in the supernatural.

Releasing Heaven will not only shatter old paradigms and outdated thought patterns on the topic of angels, Heaven, healing, and miracles, but will release sound and comprehensive biblical support, personal testimonies, heavenly encounters, and the renewing of your mind to walk by faith and not by sight. Dr. Candice teaches that every Spirit-filled believer becomes a doorway, gateway, or access point speaking of a heavenly portal here on earth to Heaven. As spiritual beings, we have been given access by the Father to ascend to the holy hills of the Lord because the veil has been torn. Through prayer and the Holy Spirit, we become gateways to Heaven where supernatural things can occur. Moreover, in *Releasing Heaven,* the author teaches the reader how to open Heaven over their lives through the power of giving, faith, obedience, being born again by the Spirit, and sowing seeds.

However, there are some Christian believers today who assume that only a select few, gifted people can operate in the supernatural or carry a special title or leadership position to release Heaven. But the Scriptures teach that *all* believers have unlimited access to the supernatural power of the Holy Spirit. You were created to host Heaven and release God's presence in your everyday affairs or sphere of activities. This time-sensitive book has been written to break false identity, fear of the supernatural, doubts of your divine purpose in God, and uproot any biblically unsupported cessationist teaching that hold the claim that the supernatural, gifts of the Spirit, angels, tongues, prophecy, heavenly encounters, and more are not for today.

After delving into the simple but life-changing pages of *Releasing Heaven,* you will discover your identity in Jesus, cultivate a heavenly mindset, and access the authority you have received in Christ Jesus. In addition, as the reader you will be able to impart more than just biblical information and knowledge but the power of impartation of Heaven with demonstration into your everyday situations and affairs. This is the key to changing, altering, and shifting atmospheres, environments, and circumstances around you by the Holy Spirit's empowerment.

Dr. Candice Smithyman has been graced with a wealth of experience in the areas of dreams, prophetic ministry, supernatural, life coaching, and leadership training. This book is a living testament and epistle of her life's work and dedication to assist believers to live transformed lives by renewing their minds with God's truth and biblical facts. *Releasing Heaven* is not just a mere book; it is a challenging, supernatural reference book and guide in moving in the Holy Spirit revelation and employment by accessing and living under an open Heaven continually.

I love the integrity and purity of this message from the author along with the practical revelation that it brings to shed light on the secret things of God. Dr. Candice's revelatory teaching, biblical application, and supportive Scriptures make this book a rarity in this hour.

Releasing Heaven will:

- Activate the faith within you to partner with Heaven to see lasting results.

- Equip you to legislate and rule in heavenly places with Christ Jesus to destroy the works and unseen powers of the devil and hell.

- Teach you how to ascend into the "Courts of Heaven" to receive breakthroughs.

- Impart fresh revelation to pray, decree, declare, and manifest the power of God.

- Encourage you to confidently enter the supernatural realm as a citizen of Heaven.

- Reveal your true spiritual identity in Christ to change the world around you.

- Empower you to release miracles by praying from a heavenly dimension.

- Upgrade you into present truth about the realms of Heaven, angels, vision, dreams, and things of the Spirit of God.

- Impart principles for accessing your heavenly riches every day.

- Renew, revive, and reignite your passion to fulfill your God-given calling.

- Begin accessing the heavenly realm to change your world today!

- Decree and declare God's prophetic promises over your life to walk in boldness.

- Change your mindset on the things of God and gain access to them immediately.

We are on the brink of Heaven invading earth, a world-changing outpouring of God's glory. But to fully encounter this requires a radical, supernatural shift in our thinking. The Body of Christ is in dire need of a heavenly revolution that I call—a Heavolution. We are called to pray *"...thy kingdom come thy will be done on earth as it is in heaven"* (Matt. 6:10).

I have the tremendous honor and privilege of fully endorsing and recommending the pages of this thought-provoking book written by Dr. Candice Smithyman. *Releasing Heaven* contains the necessary supernatural content you need to create a hub of God's presence to release Heaven on earth through you!

DR. HAKEEM COLLINS
Prophetic Voice, Author, Speaker
Author of *Heaven Declares, Prophetic Breakthrough, Command Your Healing,* and *101 Prophetic Ways God Speaks*

INTRODUCTION

I am encouraged to know that the title of this book, *Releasing Heaven: Creating A Supernatural Environment through Heavenly Encounters,* touched your heart and soul enough for you to decide to read it. This book is a culmination of years of learning how to walk in the presence of God where heavenly encounters could change our atmosphere. In this book, I share with you how to release Heaven into your environments so you sense the supernatural. I have been doing ministry since 1999 when the Lord called me to go to school and begin earning my Christian counseling degree.

I first began my journey into ministry when I was introduced to a lay counseling ministry at a non-denominational church in Whidbey Island, Washington, where my husband, Adam, and our three children were stationed. I was blessed to be a stay-at-home mother while my husband was, at that time, a Lieutenant Commander in the US Navy, running missions in the P3 plane off the coast of Whidbey Island. God began to speak to my heart at that time about the fact

He had called me into ministry and it was to be full time, so I needed to go back to college and work on a Master's degree in Christian counseling. He led me to attend Liberty University to earn my MA in Human Relations/Counseling.

After we left Whidbey, we moved to London, England. It was there that I actually began to take courses overseas through the military spouse education assistance program. This was such a blessing and opened many doors for me to begin to practice hearing the voice of God and studying how the Lord speaks to His people. In England, I studied in Birmingham with nuns, priests, and monks the practice of solitude, and my heart opened to learning to rest in the Spirit of the Lord and follow His lead. This level of quietness opened my heart to more revelation of Heaven and I began to have visions and dreams that later would become a source of communication from God about how to release Heaven in earthly atmospheres.

As I studied for my Master's degree, I put an emphasis in my studies on how the spiritual disciplines such as the discipline of solitude operates as a therapy for those with depression, anxiety, and fear. Maybe one day I will publish a book on these findings, but the more I studied solitude, the more I was healed and my ears opened up to the amazing voice of God and heavenly encounters.

Years continued to go by and more studies, even as I began to pastor Freedom Destiny Church, first in Chicago and then in Orange Park, Florida, with my husband. As we learned to step out in faith, we began to see healings and miracles, experience prophecy, and many were baptized in the Holy Spirit and with fire. People would come to our church just for a healing or to receive the baptism of the Holy Spirit, and God still sends them today.

God gave my husband and me an overload of the gift of faith and we were asked to do a variety of things that many could not explain in the natural. In this book, you will read about angel encounters, how you can create an environment of faith to see miracles and healings, how God transforms your soul, how to access heavenly treasures, and how to actually encounter the royal table in Heaven.

I have seen many amazing miracles with most not even recorded in this book, and if you can tap into an impartation of creating supernatural environments through heavenly encounters that cause you to release Heaven, then we have accomplished the goal of this book. The more of Heaven I encountered through Him touching me in my spirit, soul, and body, the more He opened doors to actually see Heaven and experience it from His perspective. Daily I can encounter Heaven and bring it to earth simply by keeping my eyes on Jesus and focusing on Him rather than the things of the world.

The things of the world will always demand your attention; but with proper training of the soul, you don't have to respond. Just because you have something crying out for you to react doesn't mean you have to respond to it. You should be responding to Heaven's call first, then God will give you the insight to access Heaven daily. When you show Him through faithfulness that He is number one, then you will see more heavenly encounters in your life.

PART I

ESTABLISHING IDENTITY FOR HEAVENLY ENCOUNTERS

CHAPTER 1

YOU ARE ETERNITY
IN ACTION

I n this chapter you will learn how you are "eternity in action." You
are eternal first and temporal second. Once you begin to get a mind
shift to this teaching, you will begin to start the foundation for seeing
your environments change through heavenly encounters.

I begin by sharing my first testimony of a heavenly encounter
when I was living in Barbers Point, Naval Air Station, in Hawaii.
My husband and I were newly married and we were stationed there. I
was 24 years old, and Adam had gone to serve in Japan on a deployment. I was all alone and diagnosed with Crohn's disease, depression,
and anxiety. The Spirit of the Lord came upon me one night—He
totally encompassed me in my sleep. I was supposed to go to a funeral
because one of the guys in my husband's squadron had died. My husband called me from Japan and said, "You have to go to this funeral."

I said, "No, I can't." I hadn't been to a funeral since my father
passed away when I was a little girl, and I just could not go.

He said, "You have to go. You're an officer's wife. You have to go out of respect for this family and be part of this."

I was like, "Oh my gosh. I do *not* want to go." I had been really suffering since my husband had been sent to Japan, leaving me in Hawaii. I was 6,000 miles away from family, and didn't know anyone. I was very lonely and afraid all the time.

The Lord began to surround me with Christians, and they began to minister to me. I shared with them, "You know what? I knew Jesus and I went to church when I was younger, and I believe in God." They said, "No, you don't know Him like this." So when God asked me to go to this funeral, I thought it was too difficult.

Well, the night before that happened, but before I was supposed to go to the funeral, I was so depressed and was sitting in from of a little black-and-white TV with a gallon of ice cream. I said, "God, if you hear me and you're there, I can't get myself out of this one." That was my pathetic prayer. "I can't get myself out of this one. I can't help myself," and I pushed aside my ice cream, fell asleep with the lights on, knowing that the next day I was going to have to get up and go to the funeral.

I woke up the next morning and I was totally pain-free. No more depression, no more anxiety. I had the greatest joy of my life. I had encountered God in the middle of the night in my sleep. Heaven had come to lay upon me. When I woke up, I thought, *God has touched me. The last prayer I prayed before I went to bed was, God, if You're there, and if You hear me, I can't get myself out of this one. I can't help myself—and He was there.* And immediately, I was healed.

I got up, dressed for the funeral, and went with a smile on my face. My friends said, "What happened to you? "

"I met Jesus. He came. He heard my prayer. He was the only One I talked to before I went to bed."

They said, "Come tonight to our Bible study." It was a good old Baptist Bible study right there on base, right at Barbers Point in Hawaii.

"Okay, really, I've never been to a Bible study before. But hey, yeah, I'll go."

When I showed up, they handed me a Bible. The pastor said, "Does anybody have anything they want to share about this particular passage?" I opened the Word of God, and immediately I had an interpretation. I was able to share with everybody what God had said. There's no way that would have happened if Heaven had not touched me. I knew in an instant what God had said in His Word when I hadn't even read His Word. I had been exposed to it as a young child, but I could not interpret it. I really could not even understand it—yet there I was with understanding.

From that point forward, my life forever changed. I visited my husband at the halfway point in his deployment in Japan. When I arrived, he took one look at me and said, "What happened to you?" I spent the week with him sharing about Jesus and how I was forever changed. I still had to fight, though, in my soul for peace many days, but through the moments of fear, anxiety, and depression, I learned to meditate and ruminate on the Word of God. I learned to work the Word until it worked for me.

Every day reciting and speaking, declaring and decreeing, and then my soul began to line up with His Word. This is how I first learned to be victorious in Christ. I learned the Word of God, which transformed my soul and made me someone who could carry the glory of the Lord and be used by Him to create supernatural environments through heavenly encounters.

We have to come to a place where we know how victorious we are. Why? Because we know we are heavenly beings and we are born again. But now, let's go dig a little deeper into Scripture where the conversation takes place with Nicodemus and Jesus. In the Gospel of John, Jesus says:

> *I have spoken to you of earthly things and you do not believe; how then will you believe if I speak of heavenly things? No one has ever gone into heaven except the one who came from heaven—the Son of Man. Just as Moses lifted up the snake in the wilderness, so the Son of Man must be lifted up, that everyone who believes may have eternal life in him* (John 3:12-15).

When Jesus speaks of eternal life, He means eternal life is heavenly life in Him. See, when you become born again in your spirit, eternity comes to reign inside you. You are literally eternity come to earth.

When you receive Jesus and become born again in your spirit, you plug into eternity so you're going to live forever. If you're going to live forever, then eternity starts today—it starts right now! Everyone who believes that Jesus Christ is our Lord and Savior is not only born again, receiving a brand-new spirit with the Holy Spirit deposited inside, we also receive a new identity. You are now considered to be a portal to Heaven; you are now a heavenly being in an earthsuit—but more than that, you are eternity in action. It's like you are a real superhero. You can call yourself, "Eternity in Action."

Eternity in Action will always open a heavenly flow because you're in eternity. Let me put it this way, when you have eternity inside you and you're a heavenly being inside, then you can say, "I like me." Come on, say it again, "I like me." Say it again, say it again! Your neighbor may not like you, but it doesn't matter, you like you, and you have a new name—Eternity in Action!

My husband laughs at me all the time and he says things like, "You like yourself, don't you?" and I respond with the biggest smile on my face, "Yes I do, I like me." Believe it or not, there was a time when I hated me. Because I can now say I like me, I know there has been a huge transformation. I hope you can wrap your head around this teaching, because you can like yourself too! You have God's DNA in you!

The Holy Spirit is inside us because we have eternity inside us; and as heavenly beings, we are portals waiting for Heaven to manifest! These are great reasons to like yourself! Now all you have to do is have the faith to allow Heaven to manifest in and through you.

Now let's go to the Gospel of John again where Jesus says, *"My kingdom is not of this world. If it were, my servants would fight to prevent my arrest by the Jewish leaders. But now my kingdom is from another place"* (John 18:36). That's literally what He meant, "My servants are still too babyish, they cannot fight with the Word of God, as they have no Word inside them."

Jesus knew His disciples would operate out of a fleshly place of pulling out their swords. In Matthew 26:52, Peter pulled out a sword, and Jesus said, *"Put your sword back in its place, for all who draw the sword will die by the sword."* Jesus felt His Kingdom was from another place, it was heavenly. You need to personally understand that your Kingdom is from another place. You are Eternity in Action.

Jesus knew He was a heavenly portal, and you are now one also. Your Kingdom is from another place.

In Hebrews the Word says, *"Therefore, since we are receiving a kingdom that cannot be shaken..."* (Heb. 12:28). Well guess what, your kingdom cannot be shaken. Don't you think that brings a lot of peace? I know you may think your house is being shaken right now. I know you may have a lot of spiritual warfare attacking you, and the enemy is waiting outside the door to destroy you, but let me tell you that the Kingdom of God cannot be shaken. Why? It's His Kingdom and He says, *"...let us be thankful, and so worship God acceptably with reverence and awe"* (Heb. 12:28). So basically, this means the Kingdom cannot be shaken so just be thankful, worship God in reverence and awe because our God is a consuming fire. Let me say it this way if I were to be so bold, God's going to come against the thing that's coming against you. So, your kingdom is not of the world—it cannot be shaken.

Now let me teach you something about Jesus and give you another reinforcement for why you are a heavenly portal. Let's go to Matthew:

> *Then Jesus came from Galilee to the Jordan to be baptized by John. But John tried to deter him, saying, "I need to be baptized by you, and do you come to me?" Jesus replied, "Let it be so now; it is proper for us to do this to fulfill all righteousness." Then John consented. As soon as Jesus was baptized, he went up out of the water. At that moment heaven was opened, and he saw the Spirit of God descending like a dove and alighting on him. And a voice from Heaven said, "This is my Son, whom I love; with him I am well pleased"* (Matthew 3:13-17).

We know that water baptism is an outward expression of an inward change that happens to you when you become born again, right? When you receive Jesus as your Lord and Savior, at that moment in time the Word says you get a new spirit. So, when you agree to be water baptized, you're saying, "I'm going to tell the rest of the world that I'm new inside. I want to tell the rest of the world that I'm Eternity in Action, that I'm a heavenly being with an earth-suit! I'm going to make a proclamation that I have repented and in me is the glory of God. I'm a brand-new person!" That's what water baptism means.

Now, what we need to know and understand from this scenario is what is said between John and Jesus. When Jesus says, in essence, *"Listen, this is what needs to be done so that all righteousness is fulfilled,"* He didn't mean that the act of water baptism led to some additional righteousness that you don't already have inside you. What Jesus meant by that statement is that you are righteous the moment you ask Jesus to come into your life, the moment that you become born again and confess your sins and receive forgiveness, then you receive a new spirit. In this one moment, you receive all the holiness and righteousness of God, all packed into one.

You may look at yourself every day and say, "This can't be true, don't you know what I just did?" Yes, but that's not what Jesus is looking at because that's the soul, that's part of the earthsuit, the place that is in transformation. Jesus wants you to begin to look at what happened to you deep inside, in your spirit first. When Jesus gave His life on the Cross and died, then was buried and resurrected, it was so that righteousness could be fulfilled in us. He was saying, "Look, I'm performing an act that will show everyone that you're made righteous when you believe in Me as your Lord and Savior. At that time you receive Me as your Lord and Savior, that is when an open Heaven comes over you."

The Scriptures are so intricate in the very way that Jesus will do certain things, but at that moment is when He walked under an open Heaven and everything you see that He does from this point forward is Him walking in an open Heaven *for you*. It's straight from the moment you receive Jesus as your Lord and Savior that you become the open Heaven portal and the miracles then begin to flow with your life.

But you do have a choice as to whether or not you're going to believe this to be true about yourself. Just because you may be acting improperly doesn't mean that you're not Eternity in Action on this earth. You don't lose your identity or position just because you make mistakes.

The enemy wants to tell you you're disqualified even after you've received Jesus as your Lord and Savior. The enemy will say things like, "You're disqualified, don't you know what you did yesterday? You're disqualified because of what you thought about the last hour." Why does he do this? It's because this robs you of your Power Source because guilt and shame set in and you won't step out and be a portal for Heaven if you are in fear of judgment from the Lord. We only disqualify ourselves when we're not living by faith through grace in our salvation being from Jesus alone.

The fact of the matter is that if the change is really made inside of you, then God has truly empowered you, and He will gain a greater joy and even a greater increase on earth if you begin to see yourself that way. When you respond in faith about who God says you are, then you shut out the enemy and you say, "But I know who I am because I know who I've accepted."

DECLARE AND DECREE TRUTH

We have to stand in faith on who we are, even in the worst of times that we may have contributed to or even caused. All we have to do is stop ourselves and say, "I know who I am and I'm acting as Eternity in Action. I'm going to allow God to operate so the open Heaven can come right now. I'm going to decree and declare that this atmosphere that I'm living in will change right now." Things may look miserable, people are complaining, stuff is going down in this house, but God just needs somebody to decree and declare and establish the thing that He wants to see happen.

You're the agent of change that's going to make that happen. But if today you want to step back and say, "You know what, I screwed up yesterday, I can't possibly be a gateway to Heaven." Then you leave God no choice but to look for somebody else who is going to say, "I'll get over myself and be the open Heaven today that these people need." Somebody needs the open Heaven around them and you are it. You are the gateway. It is a lot of responsibility, but it's also something that can open for us all kinds of blessings that we cannot even imagine pouring into the worst of situations—if we are willing to stand by faith in the substance of who we are in the Lord as Eternity in Action.

We must change our thinking. If we're going to operate cumulatively, all of us together, under an open Heaven, that means the Body of Christ will be making an enormous impact on the world. Enormous impact is when we operate as open portals for Heaven anywhere we are at any time, especially when we are receiving power from the Holy Spirit and allowing God to move freely. When we're scattered all around the world, we have a huge effect worldwide, don't we? But this means we must believe who and what we are—heavenly portals for God.

As you learn to become an open Heaven in the world, others will tap into Heaven because you were there. They will be responding, "Wow, I'm tapping into Heaven right now. I know I'm seeing something that I should not be seeing. I have hope now when I didn't have hope. I have peace now when I didn't have peace." Why? Because you agreed to believe by faith you are a heavenly portal and Eternity in Action as you operate to allow an open Heaven flow to earth through you.

There were certain things that the ancients knew who practiced walking in open Heaven encounters that I'd like to reveal. Don't you love the mysteries of God? One of the things that we have to learn is that we must rest in the sanctification of our mind. What that means is when you become born again, you have the mind of Christ. I know you don't think godly things sometimes, but by faith, you have the mind of Christ according to First Corinthians 2:16. Therefore, what you need to do every day is to sanctify your mind by telling yourself that you are a heavenly being stationed here on earth; Ask God to sanctify your mind and your heart and also your thoughts so that what you think and what you say and what you do is from Him and is by faith. If you pray these prayers over yourself, you will begin to believe who you really are. Then when you are faced with situations, you will respond as who you really are.

MIND SHIFT

The challenge I put before you is: Will you step out in faith and begin to pray over your mind and begin to operate in the realms of Heaven? If you are willing, what you're saying is, "It doesn't matter what I thought about or what I did, I'm going to believe that I'm really Eternity in Action walking, and so I'm going to pray these prayers. I'm going to decree these things. I'm going to declare this truth over my life." It is truth; it's not fact. The fact is you had an ugly thought, but the truth of the matter is that you can wash it in the Word of God.

If you will begin to transform your mind to the truth of who you are, you will begin to operate in the realm of the open Heaven. Everyday meditations lead to manifestations. I want you to say, "Meditation leads to manifestation." But make no mistake, the meditation that I'm talking about is repeating the Word of God over you on a continual basis, declaring it to yourself, speaking it to yourself, and believing it for yourself which then produces a manifestation or an action.

So, sit down and pray and ask God to sanctify your mind. Believe me, you can ask Him that because you're brand-new, holy, and righteous inside. He wants your mind to be an operation of what's going on in your spirit. After you pray these prayers, ask God to show you what He wants you to see—what is holy and righteous and good—and you'll be on your way to experiencing a manifestation that day!

You see, most of the time we don't tap into Heaven because our minds are so full of garbage, and we think to ourselves, *How am I ever going to get to Heaven when I've got all this garbage in my mind?* And I don't mean Heaven as an eternal place, I mean the heavenly peace of God in this moment and the ability for God to be able to use you in this moment, here on earth.

You may be thinking, *It can't possibly happen because my head is so full of garbage.* I have ruminating thoughts all the time that are depressing, anxious, overwhelming, and telling me that life is too much for me. However, if you pray that prayer first thing in the morning and continually throughout the day, all of a sudden you'll begin to believe that you don't have the problems you thought you did and you'll start walking in the open Heaven. Other people will begin to notice. So, when you pray the prayer and begin to allow God to show you what your next manifestation or action is, something incredible happens—you begin to operate in it!

Let us now pray for sight in this place and for the ability to believe God that you have the mind of Christ and that your mind can be sanctified. God wants you to see the things that He wants you to see, and that you are not held back by the devil and his lies and your last ungodly thought. The enemy wants to stop you from stepping into an open Heaven! He knows you're already open Heaven material; he knows you are Eternity in Action. He already knows you're all these things, but you haven't caught up with what he knows about you so he likes to throw you darts. He tells you that you're not who you say you are so he can shut you down. Then the open Heaven won't be able to operate because you won't have the faith to believe who you are in the moment.

Am I talking to you right now? If I am, then I urge you to cut off the devil by saying, "I have your game, devil. You want to shut me down, so you're telling me things that aren't the truth about me and making me hang on to that all day long, and then I won't be able to walk in the power of God or the open Heaven that God asked me to walk in. God made me a portal for Heaven, but I can't walk in it because I'm too wounded, because you have a hold of me!"

When you pray and you sanctify your mind and you ask God to show you what that next thing is, I'm telling you, He's going to show you something beautiful! He's going to tell you to get up and go talk to your spouse after you had a fight. He's going to tell you to speak nicely to your children. God is going to tell you to get up and go bless someone, even someone you don't like. I hope you get what I am saying here. It takes faith to overcome the lies of the enemy and walk like a gateway, a portal to Heaven.

When you begin to understand walking under an open Heaven, you're going to turn your house upside down, your marriage, your workplace, your church, anywhere you go. You are going to decree and declare Heaven to come in and invade the atmosphere over what's happening in your life! And you're not going to be afraid; and you're not going to cower because you already have the game plan. You've sanctified your mind and now you know the next thought is righteous from God, and you're going to get up and move on it.

Can I count on you to say you're going to do this today? This chapter is so important because of what God's imparting to you. He is helping me to articulate some of what you may think and feel so that you know someone understands you.

We as God's children are saturated with open Heaven opportunities everywhere in our lives. When you get a cup of coffee with somebody and sit and chat, that's an open Heaven. When you're with the kids, it's an open Heaven moment. What I'm trying to say is—be aware of every open Heaven opportunity. We know there's an open Heaven in the sanctuary in your church. You yourself are a heavenly portal, Eternity in Action, and where you are, Heaven is also!

CHAPTER 2

YOU CAN RELEASE HEAVEN

Sometimes people think that walking under an open Heaven is only an occasional experience or only for the elite, spiritual giants of the faith. I thought the same thing until God began to reveal to me that open Heaven encounters were for all people and come from the essence of walking in the power of knowing who we are in Christ. Because Jesus walked in open Heaven encounters, so can we.

When we use the term, "open Heaven encounters" we think of creative miracles, healings, demonic forces fleeing, peace and joy entering a room or atmosphere. Does God really want us all to walk in these powers and experiences? Yes, He does! See what He says in the Gospel of Mark:

> *He said to them, "Go into all the world and preach the gospel to all creation. Whoever believes and is baptized will be saved, but whoever does not believe will be condemned. And these signs will accompany those who believe: In my name, they will drive out demons; they*

will speak in new tongues; they will pick up snakes with their hands; and when they drink deadly poison, it will not hurt them at all; they will place their hands on sick people, and they will get well" (Mark 16:15-18).

This means you as a child of God, as a disciple of the Most High God. All this mentioned in Mark 16:15-18 happens under an open Heaven. An open Heaven is made manifest when we choose to live as though we are gateways to Heaven, or portals for the glory of God to be made manifest on earth today.

The first step is mind transformation. We must renew our minds to this truth. In this book, I take you on a journey of grabbing hold of the power that you have available in order to release Heaven into your atmospheres. The best part? It all begins with a changed mind. If you believe you have the power, then you do! God will empower you through His Word to walk these truths out until you have the confidence to change the atmospheres you're part of and influence the world around you. Are you ready to release Heaven?

THE STORY BEGINS WITH A BUILDING CAMPAIGN

This book was in process during a very important time in the history of Freedom Destiny Church where my husband and I pastor in Orange Park, Florida. It was a challenging time, but one in which we learned how to walk under an open Heaven daily. We had been faced with both trials and joys to complete a project that God had for us to take back some ungodly territory and put His name on it.

It all began when our church grew almost exponentially. At the time, we had a 10,000-square-foot facility as well as a small harvest of young people, so we had been looking high and low in our local area for a suitable piece of property. We had our hearts set on a campus that not only had a church building but also a gym and a school. We found a foreclosed property, so we decided to make an offer on the building from the funds raised from a building campaign. Sadly, we were turned down for a loan, so we began seeking God about where He wanted us to go.

Originally, we wanted a different property, but it was occupied at the time we were trying to get into the foreclosed church property. As it turned out, for the last eighteen years it had operated as a local bar. Imagine that, a church going into a bar! Nevertheless, God had called us to pray for this place for five years.

After we were turned down by the bank, the Lord opened an opportunity for us to possess another property, which was a 33,000-square-foot facility that had a total of three bars inside. We had marched around it five years before and claimed the property for Jesus, but no movement had been made since then. So, our hearts were set on the foreclosed church property.

The landlords of the bar property kept renting it to bar proprietors, and we never had enough money to acquire it. But after we were rejected for the loan, we called the landlord of the bar facility. He said the renters were leaving and they were getting ready to rent to a larger big-box retailer that had signed a lease, and demolition had even started. I told them we were inquiring because we had tried for another foreclosed property but did not have enough funds to guarantee the loan. That was Friday night.

The following Monday morning he called me and said, "I talked to the landlord, and the property is yours. We will give you the key and you can start to build now." So, we did. It was a miracle for us and the church. We had wanted and were contending for the property for five years and had even talked to the landlord years before but didn't have funds at that time—so we knew this was God directing our steps.

CONSTANT SPIRITUAL WARS

We immediately started the project demolition and then one spiritual war after another took over. It was beyond understanding. Daily spiritual warfare broke loose on this project. Were it not for my husband, Adam, the pastor of the church, we never would have made the move. As a congregation, we ended up building the whole facility ourselves, with the oversight of a general contractor. When taking territories for the Lord, there are often many spiritual battles, but God gave us victory every time.

So why is this relevant to walking under an open Heaven? Well, God will give us amazing encounters with His Spirit as the result of our unity and hard work on any project. On the day I received a revelation about writing this book to share the story, we saw visions of doves sitting all along the roof of the building we acquired only by our faith and our action. God had been wanting to engulf our new building, and this was now His entry point and His gateway to an open Heaven.

We saw miracles, healings, angels, power come upon many for the baptism of the Holy Spirit, and power came upon the weak and tired. Revival fire would come upon us so we could finish the task at hand through our fatigue, since we were building it ourselves. Every time the job slowed down and progress began to stagnate, we would all intercede and hearts would be revived and we would continue the project. We saw angels congregate in our media room in the back of the building night and day to stand guard and keep the place safe while we were battling to hold on to it. God sent people to come in and help us for a few months and to give their skills for the project, then they were gone. It took Gideon's army to build it, but only some would sustain it.

Walking in an open Heaven will open realms of possibility in the supernatural that you have never ever experienced before. It's very exciting. I want to share with you some Scriptures that will prepare you not only as an individual but also as His corporate body, as the Kingdom of Heaven on earth operating through us. When the world-wide corporate Church of Jesus Christ becomes local churches that sit under the open Heaven of God, we will see such amazing things start to happen in the lives of people near and far.

We now often look for miracles, some taking the form of radical healing miracles as in limbs growing back, people getting out of wheelchairs, and just seeing the awesome healing power of God move among the people. But one miracle that consistently happens is when God's Church body is radically transformed daily through the people who realize the open Heaven is for them.

Because you are reading this book, it means you must want more transformation in your life or you may want to be a carrier of transformation into somebody else's life. When you witness transformation in someone's thinking, that is a miracle! You can go to other places, other churches, other realms, and people aren't always walking in transformation. But since you're reading this, I know you want to be somebody who is manifesting God's truth. I am so beyond excited to teach you how to open the portals of Heaven, to give you access to this amazing transformation power!

YOU HAVE ACCESS

One way that the heavens are opened is with tithes and offerings. If you want to see an open Heaven, you need to have a heart of giving—and what better way to practice this than the discipline of giving in tithes and special monthly offerings. I'm going talk about how to open Heaven's bounty as reflected in Malachi 3:10-12.

At my church, every January we bring a first fruit offering into the house, and throughout the year any time something new happens and we experience increase. God says this specifically in Malachi:

> *"Bring the whole tithe into the storehouse, that there may be food in my house. Test me in this," says the Lord Almighty, "and see if I will not throw open the floodgates of heaven and pour out so much blessing that there will not be room enough to store it"* (Malachi 3:10).

In other words, the blessings of Heaven are poured out when we give and when we sow. Why, you ask? Because that is when we open the doorway of faith; and without faith, there can be no operation of blessing coming down from Heaven. All blessing that comes from Heaven comes through faith, because faith is the substance of things hoped for. Yes, faith is actually a real, solid evidential thing. But when God says, "I'm going to pour out an open Heaven upon this house," we must give of ourselves, our time, talent, treasure, and testimony.

That is what we did with our building, and God blessed us not only with a beautiful facility but with countless open Heaven encounters. Let's take a look at what Proverbs says, *"Honor the Lord with your wealth, with the firstfruits of all your crops; then your barns will be filled to overflowing, and your vats will brim over with new wine"* (Prov. 3:9-10). This speaks not only of the barns of your church, but your own personal barn as well. You are now a temple and Heaven wants to live within you, bringing in miracles right where you are standing.

It comes with a heart to give to the Kingdom of Heaven on earth in every moment of our lives. This kind of heart is a heart of faith giving. This is what is said of faith in Hebrews, *"Now faith is confidence in what we hope for and assurance about what we do not see. This is what the ancients were commended for"* (Heb. 11:1-2).

An open Heaven is the response that comes from the kind of heart that obeys God and gives to Him wholeheartedly by faith. Giving is an everyday option for you. It's available to you any time, even more so than coming into the house of the Lord and giving. You have opportunities to give anytime, any day, anywhere, to anyone God lays on your heart or that you have free will to give to. Right? This is not only with just tithes and offerings, this is anything in your life, anything that you give: time, talent, treasure, and your testimony.

It's also anything that you give to another human being—a smile, a touch, a look, an encouragement, anything that comes from you is an opportunity for an open Heaven to fall on you at that time. Why? Simply put, because you're engaging by faith with the elements that God gives us in His Word about the power of giving to another person. The *power* in giving will always open Heaven on earth.

Now, let me tell you a little bit of my own thinking in my own growth and development in the area of an open Heaven. I used to think that an open Heaven experience was an occasional thing and only came at a certain time, so I ended up looking and waiting and watching for occasional open Heaven opportunities. In which case, I knew at the time that the Holy Spirit was going to be flowing in such a way that there was going to be a great operation of His Spirit.

Here's my question for you, do you think like this? Are open Heaven encounters only occasional, or can they be anytime, anywhere, and frequent?

WE NEED MIND TRANSFORMATION

I want to change your thinking because God really challenged me on this truth. He began to show me that it's not so much about a one-time experience as it is that an open Heaven exists in any area at any time, no matter how disastrous the circumstance might look. You don't have to be in corporate worship in a church with hands lifted high for an open Heaven to be evident. You can be in one of the worst situations you've ever been in, but because you're there, open Heaven is there because you are the gateway to Heaven.

This means that we have to transform our minds. We must live in the realm of transformation every day of our lives. When you look at things that are going on in and around you, the last thing you're thinking about is the fact that you're a heavenly portal and that an open Heaven can exist in this situation. But it should be the *first* thing.

The truth is, in difficult times, we're going pick up our swords of complaining, anger, resentment, bitterness, whatever our vice happens to be, and that's going to be the first thing we go for. That's what our natural senses want to do. But God says we are to open our hearts to declare and decree:

> *You will also declare* [decree] *a thing, and it will be established for you; so light will shine on your ways* (Job 22:28 NKJV).

Now, if we were to whip out our own personal swords, they would be full of fleshly responses like anger, manipulation, and control tactics. But when we wield the Word of God, which is a righteous and holy sword, and we decree a thing, it will be established to us and light will shine on it. In other words, Heaven will shine on it, but it takes practice and transformation of the mind to realize we don't need to pull out our own swords, but instead go to God's Word as His sword.

Of course, there is "fact and truth." Fact is when you're looking at a situation and it doesn't look so good, and you begin to pull out your sword or fleshly means to deal with that fact. However, the fact of the matter is, it's only *truth* that comes by faith and is established to declare and decree something that will change the circumstance and bring down an open Heaven. The truth of the matter is that we are earthly beings who walk in fact, but what we need to be walking in is *truth*.

So when you sharpen your sword, you have to sharpen your sword as in the truth of the Word of God and every situation in your life. This means everything that God revealed to you in your promise to come is dependent upon what you choose to declare and decree based on the vision God gave you of what is coming ahead for you. Stop basing truth on the facts of your current circumstance.

To walk in an open Heaven over something means that all of God's blessings are about ready to come upon that thing. However, God will not bless what you decide to coerce and manipulate for your own means, using your own sword. He's only going to meet you with an open Heaven when you declare and decree the truth of the Word of God, which is the tool that will indeed bring down the open Heaven.

YOU MUST BE BORN OF THE SPIRIT

The main key to walking in open Heaven experiences is you have to be born again and literally understand mentally that you are a new creature and all the old has passed away. You have been given a new spirit when you become born again. This means you are new and whole inside and you are complete and full already. Being born again in your spirit makes you the gateway to Heaven because your new spirit is your new identity in Christ. Your soul, which is made up of your mind, your will, and your emotions, is in constant transformation so you understand that indeed you are a new creature in Christ.

In the last chapter, I mentioned the dialogue between Jesus and Nicodemus as important to understand the truth about being born again. Let's look at this passage again, as it is essential that you grasp this if you intend to walk in an open Heaven every day of your life. You must really know who you are and who is inside you in order for an open Heaven to come upon you at any moment. There is an element of confidence you must walk in, and understanding this truth is pertinent to that.

Let's take a look at what the Gospel of John says:

> *Now there was a Pharisee, a man named Nicodemus who was a member of the Jewish ruling council. He came to Jesus at night and said, "Rabbi, we know that you are a teacher who has come from God. For no one could perform the signs you are doing if God were not with him." Jesus replied, "Very truly I tell you, no one can see the kingdom of God unless they are born again." "How can someone be born when they are old?" Nicodemus asked. "Surely they cannot enter a second time into their mother's womb to be*

born!" Jesus answered, "Very truly I tell you, no one can enter the Kingdom of God unless they are born of water and the Spirit. Flesh gives birth to flesh, but the Spirit gives birth to spirit" (John 3:1-6).

Because the Spirit gives birth to spirit, if we want to see an open Heaven, it has to be the Spirit of God inside us that brings forth the open Heaven. Let me break it down; it's like one plus one equals two, right? The flesh is not going to bring about a thing of the Spirit; only the Spirit is going to bring about a move of the Holy Spirit in which an open Heaven is going to come.

Initially, all of us must be born again to walk in open Heaven encounters. It's very simple to be born again; a passage in Romans explains it very well:

If you declare with your mouth, "Jesus is Lord," and believe in your heart that God raised him from the dead, you will be saved. For it is with your heart that you believe and are justified, and it is with your mouth that you profess your faith and are saved (Romans 10:9-10).

We are all sinners; we all miss the mark; we've all made mistakes; we're all in need of a Savior; and we must believe in our heart and confess with our mouth that Jesus Christ is our Lord and Savior. All we have to do is say, "Father, please forgive me, I have sinned and I want You to come and live in my heart." That's all you have to do to be born again.

Once that happens, the unregenerate or the old self inside you becomes new; and with the new self inside, the Holy Spirit is deposited into that new self. Then, bingo, you are now a heavenly being with an earthsuit. It happens that fast! Begin now to view yourself differently—you're a heavenly being with an earthsuit. We are born in the DNA of God and He is a heavenly being, so you are a heavenly being.

When that earthsuit comes off one day and is laid down, you will still look like you look, but you will be in a spiritual body. God sees you that way today, even though you look at yourself and you see your flesh. So in order for open Heaven experiences to happen in and around us, we have to transform our minds to believe that we're heavenly beings all the time. The apostle Paul says, *"But our citizenship is in heaven. And we eagerly await a Savior from there, the Lord Jesus Christ"* (Phil. 3:20).

I'm not just a heavenly being when good things are going on around me and I have those little goose bumps and all that. No, that's not only when I'm a heavenly being. I'm also a heavenly being when things are really bad and I'm experiencing pain and my soul is out of whack and I am struggling and depressed and anxious. I am still a heavenly being!

You need to take authority over those feelings. How? By faith knowing that you are a heavenly being! If you have not faith in who you really are, then those things are not going to change. All you're doing is struggling with yourself and getting no victory at all.

Understanding these truths mentioned in this chapter is the beginning of realizing we have a new identity in Christ. True manifestations from Heaven are catapulted by people who understand their identity as being heavenly beings first. Let's go on to the next chapter and learn more about your identity as a citizen of Heaven.

CHAPTER 3

GATEWAY TO HEAVEN

O ne Wednesday night service at my church, Freedom Destiny, the power of God came in to minister mightily to the young people. God had spoken to my heart that He wanted them to come and drink from His well.

It was during the month of Iyar on the Hebrew calendar, and literally a time when in the spirit realm we were remembering how the Israelites were released from their bondage and going forward to the Promised Land. You can read the story in Exodus chapters 13–18. They were in the wilderness and God wanted to open the wells of Heaven and bring water for His people. The Word says,

> *The whole Israelite community set out from the Desert of*
> *Sin, traveling from place to place as the Lord commanded.*
> *They camped at Rephidim, but there was no water for the*
> *people to drink. So they quarreled with Moses and said,*
> *"Give us water to drink." Moses replied, "Why do you*
> *quarrel with me? Why do you put the Lord to the test?"*

But the people were thirsty for water there, and they grumbled against Moses. They said, "Why did you bring us up out of Egypt to make us and our children and livestock die of thirst?" Then Moses cried out to the Lord, "What am I to do with these people? They are almost ready to stone me." The Lord answered Moses, "Go out in front of the people. Take with you some of the elders of Israel and take in your hand the staff with which you struck the Nile, and go. I will stand there before you by the rock at Horeb. Strike the rock, and water will come out of it for the people to drink." So Moses did this in the sight of the elders of Israel. And he called the place Massah and Meribah because the Israelites quarreled and because they tested the Lord saying, "Is the Lord among us or not?" (Exodus 17:1-7)

So that night at our church, God opened the rock and His Holy Spirit called forth the young people from 12-18 years of age to come to the altar. We began to lay hands on them; so many were restricted and bound. God ministered healing and many received the baptism of the Holy Spirit.

Then I looked over and I saw the elementary kids had been brought into the sanctuary. One of the pastors had brought them to come and receive. God again released His Spirit and an open Heaven came to give them refreshment and revival. For the remainder of the night the adults and children worshipped the Lord and we had an impartation to be sent forth to go and make disciples. It was a powerful display of an open Heaven.

Why did that happen? Because God spoke and we did not listen to what the environment was saying about dryness in the people;

rather, we listened to God and did exactly what He said, which was to lay hands on the youth.

Normally we follow the routine service, but this time God said, "I want to touch My people a different way." The way God touched His people was through us, His people, the gateways to Heaven. He wanted us to open ourselves to the glory and not have an agenda—He wanted us to let Him do His thing. I have seen many encounters with God like this and our church has been in revival for short stints many times. I share this story because it showed that some people had to throw out their routine agenda if they wanted to see God move and have the confidence to know God was calling them.

You have to have confidence God is asking you to be the portal for the change and to be so focused on Him that you don't look to your environment or people for affirmation or for confirmation that you heard from God on this change. People are thirsty and tired themselves and they would not know how or where to go to get the water unless you were the one God chose to lead them there. God chose Moses to strike the rock and begin the flow. Is He calling you to stop listening to the grumbling of those you lead and begin to do as God says and strike the rock and let the water flow?

You are the heavenly portal He wants to use to create an environment for Heaven to show up. God creates an environment when you determine to keep your focus on Him and stop looking at the environment for approval or affirmation. You are to be the one God uses to change the situation, not just the one needing approval or sensing if it will change. Just do what He says and He will change the environment—and salvations, healings, and miracles will happen all in His name!

One of the weak areas of the Church of Jesus Christ today is that it does not realize its full potential and does not know that the Ecclesia is the gateway to Heaven on earth. As members of Christ's body, we really need to grasp this concept of how important we are to Heaven. So in order to probe this realization and make it practical on earth, we need to ask ourselves these two questions: 1) How am I the gateway to Heaven; and 2) How does this gateway operate?

In this chapter, I reveal that you are a gateway to Heaven. Do you know that you are the gateway to Heaven, or does this sound crazy? Believe it; you *are* the gateway between Heaven and earth. You *are* the one who has the key.

In Chapter 1, I mentioned that Jesus said this in John, *"I've spoken to you of earthly things and you do not believe. How then will you believe if I speak of heavenly things?"* (John 3:12). He's saying there's a big difference between earth and Heaven, and we know that. He says there are things He wants to reveal to us, but even when He's spoken of earthly things, we still don't quite get it.

Every year we get smarter, and we will receive more revelation from Heaven. We go from glory to glory to glory. We will see more and more of the glory of God coming upon us and activating our minds so that we can step into an understanding of heavenly things. But since we don't understand heavenly things, there's going to be a struggle in the earthly realm for this revelation to become part of who we are. This is my desire for you as you read this book—that this truth becomes more evident to you and Heaven becomes more real and less subjective, yet very reachable.

JACOB'S LADDER

In the next few chapters I discuss Jacob and his heavenly encounter in Genesis 28 so you can begin to understand how to create supernatural environments from heavenly encounters. We must know how God interacted with Jacob, so I go into great depth in the text over the next few chapters, focusing only on Genesis 28 and his encounter with God at Bethel.

As you study this passage, I am believing you will become changed in your identity and begin to see yourself as God's house for the manifestation of miracles, healings, and power to flow through you as a glory portal or gateway to Heaven. In the following Scripture passage, Jacob was made consciously aware of a pathway to Heaven because of a dream.

Jacob left Beersheba and set out for Harran. When he reached a certain place, he stopped for the night because the sun had set. Taking one of the stones there, he put it under his head and lay down to sleep. He had a dream in which he saw a stairway resting on the earth, with its top reaching to heaven, and the angels of God were ascending and descending on it. There above it stood the Lord, and he said: "I am the Lord, the God of your father Abraham and the God of Isaac. I will give you and your descendants the land on which you are lying. Your descendants will be like the dust of the earth, and you will spread out to the west and to the east, to the north and to the south. All peoples on earth will be blessed through you and your offspring. I am with you and will watch over you wherever you go, and I will bring you back to this land. I will not leave you until I have done what I have promised you." When Jacob awoke from his sleep, he thought, "Surely the Lord is in this place, and I was not aware of it" (Genesis 28:10-16).

In this dream, Jacob sees angels ascending and descending. He sees the Lord standing above the stairway from his dream state. But when he wakes up from his sleep, he says, "Wow, God is here and I didn't know it." Do you know that God can be ever present, but we may not be cognizant of His presence, even though He is present with us?

In this passage, Jacob shares his revelation that he was completely unaware of God's presence. What does that mean? He is saying, I did not perceive nor see that I was in a place where God was in operation. In the Word it says of Jacob, *"He was afraid and he said, 'How awesome is this place! This is none other than the house of God; this is the gate of heaven'"* (Gen. 28:17).

YOUR MIND IS A GATEWAY

Now, let me break this down. You may not have had a dream while your head is resting on a rock, where you see angels ascending and descending, and see the throne of God along the top of it. But, just like Jacob, you do have an awareness about you. You have a mind that is a portal to the gateway of Heaven. Your mind is a portal in which Heaven comes through and operates. Your mind is a place that is a gate, in which Heaven has the opportunity to manifest on earth.

Jesus came to tabernacle with us, and you indeed are the temple of the Holy Spirit (see 1 Cor. 6:19). You are the tabernacle in which the Spirit of God resides. Your mind, and how clearly you think about Heaven and about heavenly things, opens the opportunity for Heaven to have a portal through which its power can be activated on earth. It's through your mind and it's through what you believe!

When you believe and when you understand this, you're a walking gateway to Heaven. That's very important. When you look at yourself as a gateway to Heaven itself, keeping your focus and keeping your eye on Him, you can be used by God in any instance. Remember how Jacob had said, *"How awesome is this place! This is none other than the house of God. This is the gate of heaven"* (Gen. 28:17). Listen to what he is saying—first he was not *aware* of the fact that God was in this place, but now he *is* aware. Right? This is when he receives the revelation. Wow, this is none other than the house of God.

When we ourselves get a revelation of the fact that the Spirit of the Lord is within us and we can keep our mind's eye on the Lord and what He wants to do, we can then open ourselves up to be the gateway to Heaven. But we absolutely have to have an eye on Him. Just like Christian music artist Toby Mac sings in his song, *"Eye on It,"* we have to have an eye on Him, our mind's eye.

No matter what you're doing, you have to have a cognizant understanding of the fact that God is with you in this moment, and that He wants to do something. Then you've opened yourself up to being a portal Heaven can activate. But when you don't live like that, you begin to live too much in the world, and you get too earthly about things in your mind, so you miss the opportunity. You are unaware of the fact that you are the house of God walking, and then God can't use you in that moment of time. Heaven wanted to activate on earth, but the opportunity was overlooked, until another chance encounter comes along.

We have to drive our spiritual senses to a place where we can activate our minds to the fact that we are the house of God, and we become aware of Him again. How do you activate your mind? It's simple, you return to the spiritual disciplines. Go back to fasting, praying, reading the Word, and focusing. All of these things help you put your attention on Him. Also, corporate worship and worshipping at home by yourself. This daily lifestyle causes you to have to press in to the things of God; and when you press in, you honor the fact that you are the house of God, and you are the gateway of Heaven.

In the Book of Matthew, some heavenly revelation comes to the disciples:

> When Jesus came to the region of Caesarea Philippi, he asked his disciples, "Who do people say the Son of Man is?" They replied, "Some say John the Baptist; others say Elijah; and still others, Jeremiah or one of the prophets." "But what about you?" he asked. "Who do you say I am?" Simon Peter answered, "You are the Messiah, the Son of the living God." Jesus replied, "Blessed are you, Simon son of Jonah, for this was not revealed to you by flesh and blood, but by my Father in heaven" (Matthew 16:13-17).

In other words, knowing that Jesus is the Messiah is not an earthly thing. The disciples received this revelation from Heaven. There's no way you would have known that had My Father not told you. So, He says specifically, *"...this was not revealed to you by flesh and blood..."* (Matt. 16:17). We're not going to get cues from Heaven in flesh-and-blood situations. We're going to get cues from Heaven because we've opened our minds to hear and understand what God is saying, and we've agreed to be the gateway to Heaven.

If you go out to dinner with your family and as you're eating, you continue to remind yourself that you are a portal in which Heaven comes to earth, then when somebody needs something in this restaurant, you're going to have an understanding of what the person needs, because you've made yourself constantly aware of the fact that God might want to do something through you in this moment.

It works the same anywhere, anytime, even at a gas station, the grocery store, a coffee shop. Wherever you are, the gateway to Heaven is there also. But you have to keep your mind open, and your mind's eye focused on the Lord. You have to take a second look at your purpose. If your purpose is that you're a gateway to Heaven, which all believers are, then we live in the world but we view it from a different perspective. We view it as God wants to do something in this place, and He needs us to be the avenue to do that.

In the Book of Psalms, the Word reads:

> *Shout for joy to the Lord, all the earth. Worship the Lord with gladness; come before him with joyful songs. Know that the Lord is God. It is he who made us, and we are his; we are his people, the sheep of his pasture. Enter his gates with thanksgiving and his courts with praise; give thanks to him and praise his name. For the Lord is good and his love endures forever; his faithfulness continues through all generations* (Psalm 100:1-5).

How does it say we enter His gates? With thanksgiving! If you want to enter His gates, thank Him. For example, when you're having dinner with your family in a restaurant, you should be full of thankfulness about that experience, right? You should thank the Lord not just for the food or even for the fellowship, although those are admirable things to take into account. What you are to do is simply thank Him—because when you thank Him, your mind's eye is on Him while you're having dinner with your family. In doing so, you're now opening yourself up to be a glory portal for Heaven. You're tuned into who God is and what He wants to do. You've now become consciously aware of His presence and the gates are beginning to open. That dinner is going to get a whole lot better. And you're going to enjoy your life a whole lot more because Heaven has become part of what you're presently doing. That can happen for everybody.

I know that you want to be a gateway to Heaven. As discussed earlier, Jesus talked about another dimension when He spoke to Nicodemus in John 3. You need to grasp the same truth today—that you live in another dimension. I know you think you're in this earth-suit, and you're sitting right there reading this book and experiencing life, but technically you're in the heavenly dimension, even though you're sitting in the earthly dimension. Why? Because you will never die in your spirit if you know Jesus as your Lord and Savior.

HEAVENLY FIRST

So, because you're living now, eternity is happening right now, even though you're currently living on earth. Everybody thinks eternity is the next place we're going to live. No, eternity is right now, right in this place. We have to change our thinking. If you want to see the supernatural and live a life of miracles for God, you have to change your thinking about who you are today, in this moment. You are not an earthly being, you are a heavenly being who lives on earth. If the Church of Jesus Christ doesn't receive this revelation, we're not going to make much of a difference here in these end times we're dealing with.

What if you are somehow involved in a life crisis situation and you are the only one who knows Jesus, but you do not know how to walk in being a heavenly portal and speak life to that difficult situation? Maybe because you've never spoken life to any situation yet, you're thinking, *What good am I going to be in the midst of that crisis?* My advice? You better start practicing now when there is no crisis, because when it comes, you need to be the one God uses.

Start thinking like this, and every day of your life is going to be so much better than it is right now. Your problems are not going to look the same way. I know they may seem catastrophic, but God is bigger than your catastrophe! Having a heavenly perspective puts everything into its proper perception. As you watch terrible things happening in the world, you can get a better handle on the fact that you have power and can bring Heaven into a situation that looks very, very bad in the moment.

If you practice when you're out of season, then you will be ready for the in season. You have to get ready for the in season of troubles. God says He's training an army. How do you train an army? You train an army in bootcamp and with drills behind the scenes. You are the army of God and you are the gateway to Heaven. God wants His heavenly portals to stand up and be gateways for open Heaven manifestations.

Reframe your thinking from worldly and earthly to heavenly and spiritual. Then you will be in proper position. Jesus says in John, *"...I am the gate; whoever enters through me will be saved. They will come in and go out, and find pasture"* (John 10:9). When we become saved, we enter into the realm of eternity. At that point, we've entered into His gates, right? And at that particular point, now we have to be ready to be an open gate.

Let's take a look at some wisdom from Second Corinthians, *"For though we live in the world, we do not wage war as the world does"* (2 Cor. 10:3). The weapons we, the Ecclesia or the Church, fight with are not the weapons of the world. Because you are a gateway to Heaven, you don't operate like your neighbor does. I know your neighbor may act all crazy, but you don't have to act that way. The weapons we fight with are not weapons of the world. On the contrary, our weapons have divine power to demolish strongholds.

Your weapons can take down strongholds. Imagine that, strongholds! Everybody else's weapons are just earthly, knocking back and forth, one or the other. However, yours can demolish strongholds. Why? Because you're a gateway to Heaven and Heaven has come to demolish what's not in Heaven. *"We demolish arguments and every pretension that sets itself up against the knowledge of God, and we take captive every thought to make it obedient to Christ"* (2 Cor. 10:5).

A HEAVENLY MIND

So, where is the heavenly gate? It's your mind. If your mind can take captive every thought to Christ, then you're positioning yourself to be the gateway to Heaven. But if your mind is messing with earthly things, then you close the gate. Gate's shut. It's on lockdown. Heaven isn't coming down, and you're not going up. You can lock yourself out of Heaven, even though you're saved. You're saved, but you don't have an understanding of where you are presently because you are in an earthly realm.

People can go on lockdown all the time. But guess what? You have the key and the free will to decide if that is where you want to stay. God doesn't come and put pressure on you to be the gateway to Heaven. He just says, you are the gateway to Heaven. But you can say, "You know what? I don't feel like being Heaven today. I'm turning it off."

God says, "Really? You're turning down an opportunity to be a heavenly portal that will make a difference in you and others? Okay. Who else is out there? Oh, that person is a little responsive. Maybe I'll find cooperation there. No. I, God, am turned off in that person's mind too. I need somebody who is open to Heaven. Who is it? Over there in the back row. You're it! Thank you! You won't be sorry for your obedience. In fact, you will mature in ways you never dreamed possible."

If you're the one who opened up, all of a sudden Heaven's coming down upon you. You're the one God will use. Others locked Him out. We have to pay attention to the fact that it's really, really important that we don't lock God out from bringing Heaven to earth through us. We have to take captive every thought and make it obedient to Christ so we can respond in every crucial moment—whatever moment when Heaven wants to impact earth. In Matthew 23:13 we see Jesus speaking to those who have locked out the power of God because they have become too self-righteous and too law-driven:

> *Woe to you, teachers of the law and Pharisees, you hypocrites! You shut the door of the kingdom of heaven in people's faces. You yourselves do not enter, nor will you let those enter who are trying to* (Matthew 23:13).

Now that's a rebuke to teachers, right? That's a rebuke to the five-fold ministry and to those who bring forth the gospel message and teach and train others. We have a responsibility to teach about the Kingdom of Heaven. Teach it in such a way that people understand what the Kingdom of Heaven is, and they understand that each and every one of them are heavenly portals in their minds.

In a passage in Second Peter, Peter is telling us that God has given us great and precious promises, Peter says, *"…so that through them you may participate in the divine nature, having escaped the corruption in the world caused by evil desires"* (2 Pet. 1:4). Then in verse 12 he writes, *"So I will always remind you of these things, even though you know them and are firmly established in the truth you now have"* (2 Pet. 1:12). He's talking to the Church. Peter says in essence, "Listen, Church, I want to remind you of this. There are certain qualities that will prevent you from being productive in your knowledge of the Lord Jesus, even though you know certain things and are firmly established in the truth. I want to refresh your memory, as long as I live in this tent body."

What he is basically saying is, "Because I know that one day my body's going to be put aside," as Jesus has made clear to him, "I'm going to make every effort to see that after I leave, you will always remember these things. For we did not follow cleverly devised stories when we told you about the coming of our Lord Jesus Christ and His power, but we were eyewitnesses of His majesty."

Yes, it's true that Peter actually saw Jesus doing miracles. But it is true today that if you are the gateway of Heaven, you are people's eyewitness to Heaven manifesting right in front of them. We are the ones people are eyeballing to determine whether or not Heaven is truly real.

> *The Son is the radiance of God's glory and the exact representation of his being, sustaining all things by his powerful word. After he had provided purification for sins, he sat down at the right hand of the Majesty in heaven* (Hebrews 1:3).

The fullness of Heaven is within Him.

People are wondering, does Jesus love me? Will Jesus accept me? Will Jesus forgive me? Heaven is a welcoming place, because God sent His one and only Son to die for us so that we would be forgiven and accepted into that place. We are adopted, we are heirs, and our great inheritance was given to us by Jesus Christ by His death, burial, and resurrection. People want to know if everything you say is true. They're just waiting to see whether or not you're going to unlock the door of your mind and take every thought obedient to Christ and allow the Lord to use you in a mighty way. It's you He wants to use.

So, my question to you is this: Given what you've read about the fact that you are the gateway to Heaven, how will you change your life as a result of what you've read today? When you change your thinking to these truths, you will walk in a new realm, one of miracles, signs and wonders, healing and deliverances. People will be set free. The captives will be set free because you are there to speak life over them. There should be no death where you are, there should only be life.

But the difference between life and death is knowing the answers to these questions:

- What do you believe about God?
- What do you believe about yourself?
- What do you believe about who you are in Christ?

The right answers give you the power you need to operate as the gateway to Heaven. It's salvation, but it's also the power of the Holy Spirit, it's both of those together, all at once.

CHAPTER 4

OPEN HEAVEN
MANIFESTATIONS

In the last chapter, you learned about being a gateway to Heaven in your mind. In this chapter, we discuss more from Genesis 28 and how this revelation of being God's house can open doors for you to have heavenly encounters. The basics of being a heavenly portal start when we receive Jesus as our Lord and Savior—we become born again in the Spirit. Then we open a pathway for Heaven to manifest on earth, because all things that come from Heaven have to operate spiritually. The spiritual can operate into the natural, but there has to be a portal. There has to be a way for that to happen. You're that way! When you become born again in the Spirit, then you have connection to the spirit realm—which means you have connection to Heaven, which means you have to change your image of yourself and believe that you are first and foremost a heavenly being by nature, only existing here in an earthsuit. That's a hard one to wrap ourselves around.

YOU ARE A HEAVENLY BEING

Many people are taught from the time they were very young that they were just earthly beings, no more. Others are taught about Jesus while attending church and learn that they aren't just earthly beings. They heard that when you receive Jesus as your Lord and Savior, you become a heavenly being. You are now a citizen of Heaven (see Phil. 3:20). This means we must learn to live as heavenly beings.

Jesus knew this and He prayed a prayer for His disciples because He wanted them so much to understand the truth of the Word of God and who they were. John 17:13-18 is the prayer that He prayed for His disciples, which is the same prayer that He wants for us, so this prayer is for you.

Jesus says, *"I am coming to you now, but I say these things while I am still in the world, so that they may have the full measure of my joy within them"* (John 17:13). In other words, Jesus came so that we, His disciples, would have the full measure of His joy while we are in the world.

Continuing, Jesus says, "[Father,] *I have given them your word and the world has hated them, for they are not of the world any more than I am of the world"* (John 17:14). Now let's think about this a bit. Jesus is praying this prayer for the disciples and He is saying, "Look, those who are mine are not even of this world although they think that they are." He says, "They are not of the world any more than I am in the world." He says this while He's physically with them, which means the Holy Spirit's presence has yet to come to be manifest on earth at this point.

Jesus is talking about the fact that He is actually believing great things for the disciples. It is like He is praying, "I'm seeing them. I know what they believe. I know that they're going to be born of the

Spirit, that they're going to be connected to Me, that they're going to be connected to the heavenly realm."

Jesus says, *"My prayer is not that you take them out of the world but that you protect them from the evil one"* (John 17:15). That is Jesus' prayer for us. Not that we'd be removed from this place but that we stay here as heavenly beings in earthsuits and be protected from the evil one.

Then Jesus says, "[Father], *sanctify them by the truth; your word is truth. As you sent me into the world, I have sent them into the world"* (John 17:17-18). He's saying, "Look, I want them to see themselves the way I see them. They're not of this world, and I want You, Father, to sanctify them by the truth because Your Word is the truth." So as heavenly beings, the way we become sanctified is to live by the Word of God—that's the only way. Sanctification means that there is anointing, a purification, a cleansing of our soul that comes upon us when the truth of the Word of God is deposited inside us. Apart from the word of truth, we, as heavenly beings, have no road map to live our lives on this planet. You do not know what you are supposed to do if you do not know the Word of God.

WILL OF GOD

I hear people say all the time, "Well, what *is* the will of God?" The will of God is the Word of God. If you know *not* the Word of God, you know *not* His will. It seems believers are always looking for the will of God as though it's some type of subjective thing that God deposits in us. Yes, that is true. But there are also objective things that are God's will as well. Nevertheless, nothing is outside the objective of the Word of truth that He gives us. His will is His Word, so everything should match up with that. We must learn as heavenly beings to sanctify our souls with the Word of truth. Jesus explains that great heavenly things came the moment He arrived on earth.

Let me take you to a passage in John. It reads, *"Then Nathanael declared, 'Rabbi, you are the Son of God; you are the King of Israel.' Jesus said, 'You believe because I told you I saw you under the fig tree. You will see greater things than that'"* (John 1:49-50). In other words, there was a situation where Jesus saw Nathanael under the fig tree. When Jesus sees him, He says, *"I saw you under the fig tree."* Naturally then, Nathanael is thinking, *"Whoa, He must be the Son of God. I didn't know He saw me under the fig tree, but He's telling me He saw me under the fig tree."* Jesus added to the conversation by saying, *"You will see greater things than that."* He then added, "Very truly I tell you, you will see 'heaven open, and the angels of God ascending and descending on the Son of Man'" (John 1:50-51). So, what He is saying is this, "When I am here, when Heaven is present, the angels of God will ascend and descend on Me." Now, what would you say if I told you the same is true of you?

You see, Jesus is an example of what is for us as we stay here as His heavenly beings. If the angels of God would ascend and descend on the Son of Man while He was here, then the angels of God will ascend and descend on you if you understand that you are a heavenly portal that brings Heaven to earth when you sanctify your mind and you stand in the truth of the Word of God. You are a chosen vessel to be a glory portal.

OPEN HEAVEN NOW

People want to see the manifestations of the Holy Spirit. They want to see the manifestations of the heavenly realm. Listen, Heaven is your only hope. For us to live in this world and have no hope of Heaven is despair for us. But to wrap ourselves around the fact that we can live in Heaven and walk on the earth means that we open a portal of joy that can never be taken from us. It's a joy that fills you from the moment you receive Jesus as your Lord and Savior—and it can stay with you. You see, the enemy will come through a counterfeit and try to distract you and detract you; but the fact is, Heaven will never go away! It will never pass away, and you are part of it today on this planet. You must start thinking this way in the end times that we're in, or God will not be able to manifest Himself the way He wants to manifest Himself—through you as a heavenly portal.

Jesus knew His identity. He knew who and where He was when He said, "Listen, when I'm here, the angels will descend and ascend upon Me." That's not an arrogant statement. That is simply a statement of truth. Where Heaven is, angels will ascend and descend. Where you are, angels will ascend and descend, just like Jacob saw in Genesis 28:10-15, which we read in the last chapter. Remember that I mentioned I would teach more on this passage because it really digs deep into heavenly encounters, and I want you to understand this. So the passage is cited again for your reference:

> *Jacob left Beersheba and set out for Harran. When he reached a certain place, he stopped for the night because the sun had set. Taking one of the stones there, he put it under his head and lay down to sleep. He had a dream in which he saw a stairway resting on the earth, with its top reaching to heaven, and the angels of God were ascending and descending on it. There above it stood the Lord, and he said: "I am the Lord, the God of your father Abraham and the God of Isaac. I will give you and your descendants the land on which you are lying. Your descendants*

*will be like the dust of the earth, and you will spread out
to the west and to the east, to the north and to the south.
All peoples on earth will be blessed through you and your
offspring. I am with you and will watch over you wherever you go, and I will bring you back to this land. I will
not leave you until I have done what I have promised you"*
(Genesis 28:10-15).

What happened to Jacob is an example of an open Heaven manifestation. Jacob is a man of the flesh in the natural. He's sleeping and
he has a dream, and in this place he sees the angels of God ascending
and descending. When he wakes up from his sleep, when he comes
back to his consciousness, he says, *"Surely the Lord is in this place, and
I was not aware of it"* (Gen. 28:16). In other words, "I woke up from
my sleep but I was not consciously aware that Heaven comes down
to earth the way that I saw in my dream. But now, I, Jacob, am completely changed by this experience. I now have a conscious awareness
of Heaven."

Do you want a conscious awareness of Heaven? You can have this
too! Jacob says he was not consciously aware of God's presence. If
Jacob had no consciousness before, but now is aware and awakened
to that truth, that could be us too. Jacob went to sleep and had this
dream. Most people have dreams right and left about anything and
everything. Heaven is talking to you in your dreams. Are you writing
down what Heaven is saying to you? Are you praying and interceding
on what Heaven is speaking to you through your dreams?

Dreams are manifestations of the portal of Heaven coming to
earth through you. In a dream, Heaven could be saying to you,
"Listen, this is what's going on." And so to Jacob, the Lord was saying to him, "Listen, angels are ascending and descending in this place

and I, God, am going to do these things for you. I, God, have a promise for you." He says, "And I'm not going to leave you...." God speaks that He is going to fulfill that promise, and that promise is going to come to pass, because God is saying, "I'm with you."

When you have a heavenly experience with God, what do you know for sure? That God is with you. That is one thing you walk away from those experiences with and think, *Whoa, surely that had to have been God. God is in this place!* As this Scripture passage continues, in verse 17 it says of Jacob, *"He was afraid and said, 'How awesome is this place! This is none other than the house of God; this is the gate of heaven'"* (Gen. 28:17). Jacob has great reverence for what he experienced, so he makes a declaration in that place that Heaven had arrived. As it says in the Word, *"Declare and decree a thing"* (Job 22:28 KJV).

We must declare and decree. So here as Jacob encounters Heaven, he declares and decrees, "Look, this place is awesome. This is the house of God, the gate of Heaven." Now, I want you to declare and decree you are the house of God and the gateway of Heaven. The fact is, Jacob had a dream about a place called the house of God; but the truth of the matter is, when you come to know Jesus as your Lord and Savior, you then *become* the house of God.

THE HOUSE OF GOD

"Do you not know that your bodies are temples of the Holy Spirit, who is in you, whom you have received from God? You are not your own; you were bought at a price. Therefore honor God with your bodies" (1 Cor. 6:19-20). The price that was paid for you was the blood of Jesus on the Cross. That's the price that was paid so that you can be a temple of the Holy Spirit.

If you are indeed the house of God, then you are indeed the gateway of Heaven. We must change our thinking to believe this if we are going to activate heavenly encounters on the earth. How many believers daily think about the fact that we are portals in which Heaven comes to earth? Many just say, "Well, this might happen when I'm in church." Or, "Maybe it's over there in that place." But we won't say it's *our* place, *our* temple of the Holy Spirit that is God's place. We give credit to a place, but not to our very own personal house of God.

In Genesis 28 again, Jacob declares that this is *"the house of God; this is the gate of Heaven"* (Gen. 28:17). He has a conscious awareness. The Word says that after his declaration, Jacob takes a stone and sets it up as a pillar and pours oil on top of it. And he calls that place Bethel, though the city used to be called Luz.

When Jacob sets the stone up as a pillar, he's setting up a spiritual marker signifying that that he is now aware of the house of God. He is now aware of the fact that a change in identity has occurred in this place. What is he doing when he pours oil on the spiritual marker? He is saying this place is now anointed, sanctified, and set apart for the Lord! This place is now the house of God.

Because you are now the house of God and God says, "Sanctify yourself with the Word of truth," He's saying that you need to make sure that an identity change has been made, that you are conscious of it and that you will anoint yourself and set yourself apart and consecrate yourself so that the house of God can now be present walking around on earth in you. What do you think of that?

We have a responsibility, isn't that right? We have a responsibility now to maintain a conscious awareness of who we are as the temples of God, as the houses of God. With that means sanctification must come.

Now, listen, what's so amazing about this story is that the oil didn't go on the pillar until after the declaration was made about what this place was. You don't have to be sanctified to come enter through the doors of a church, and you don't have to be clean. You can be nuts, messed up, screwed up, drunked up, fouled up, whatever kind you are, because we all were and some of us still are that way in churches worldwide.

However, when you receive Jesus and you become the house of God, then it's time to go through the process of sanctification. It's time to then allow God to slowly but surely clean up the house so that the house can become consciously aware of the fact that you are now a heavenly being who walks on earth. Believe me when I say, God needs you now to be accessible to Him and to have an awareness of Him. If you would like a good book to read on the subject of soul transformation, I recommend the book I wrote with my husband titled, *Soul Transformation: Your Personal Journey.*[1] In it we coach you for six weeks on the process of soul transformation.

THE SANCTIFIED LIFE

If you do not live a sanctified life, God will not be accessible to you, nor you to Him. But if you are willing to go on the journey of receiving Jesus as your Lord and Savior, becoming new inside, becoming the house of God, and then saying, "I'm determined now to go through the process of soul transformation, the process of sanctification," then you are His, and throughout your life He will help you be aware of His presence and where He wants to operate in and around you.

We have to know that part of sanctification means changing our lifestyles. A few disciplines we can practice are praying, fasting, and giving. We all have something that needs to be cleaned up, and spiritual disciplines keep our focus on God and His heart. God is faithful and He will always come when His people seek His face. You can make fasting a lifestyle. Prayer should be an everyday part of your life. You should be reading the Word of Truth every day of your life.

The following is a quick and easy way to make the Word of God really useful to you if you're wondering where to begin when seeking God for soul transformation.

First, start with your problem and find out what God says about it—and you will be sanctified rather quickly. Instead of starting in the beginning of the Bible in Genesis to help you with issues, flip to the back of your Bible and look at the topical concordance. Determine your issue and then find all the Scriptures that match up with it. As you read all of the Scriptures, you will be sowing the Word of truth into your soul. Then God will begin to speak to you about the issue through His Word. This is a quick but profound way to allow God to clean you up. Nowadays you can download a good App for your phone to simply search your issue, and the App will take you to all the Scriptures that apply.

We also know that sanctification has to do with the mind because when you know who you are and when you know what you're facing and you know what kind of choices and decisions have to be made in your life, you will then begin to position yourself to be an open portal. The open portal entrance is the mind. This is why it's so important that you understand you have the mind of Christ. This is what the Word says. You have the mind of Christ, but if you're not putting it to use, it's because you haven't understood the way the mind of Christ needs to be activated in you. You have to call on the mind of Christ for activation to take place.

Before you do anything, you can pray and ask God to sanctify your mind. When you ask God to sanctify your mind, you have a whole lot greater faith knowing that your thoughts are righteous, and then you're ready to hear what the Lord has to say. Why is that? So you can be His tool or His avenue for Heaven to open above you. When the heavens are open above you, you will hear from the Lord.

Let's go to the Book of Deuteronomy to get an idea of how much of Heaven is available to you right where you are, how much of Heaven is in operation, and also what it looks like: *The Lord will open the heavens, the storehouse of his bounty, to send rain on your land in season and to bless all the work of your hands..."* (Deut. 28:12).

When Heaven is activated in your life, you will see plenty and blessings, and the work of your hands will be blessed. *"...You will lend to many nations but will borrow from none"* (Deut. 28:12). In other words, you'll lend to people but you will be financially upright and not have to borrow from them.

> *The Lord will make you the head, not the tail. If you pay attention to the commands of the Lord your God that I give you this day and carefully follow them, you will always be at the top, never at the bottom* (Deuteronomy 28:13).

We will always be on top. But here's the danger. He says in the next verse, *"Do not turn aside from any of the commands I give you today, to the right or to the left, following other gods and serving them"* (Deut. 28:14). That is the warning after all of the open Heaven blessings. Why? Because God says the danger is falling in love with another god. When that happens, Heaven's blessing stops flowing.

When you're dealing with issues in and around your life and you have an attraction to that thing, it becomes a god in your life. That god is distracting you and detracting you from the open Heaven blessings that God wants to bring to you. Until you recognize your connection with that other god, you won't be able to break free and the open Heaven blessings will cease. You'll find in those situations you are not the head—you are the tail. You will find out that you are asking for things from others instead of being the one who gives to them. Everything turns upside down.

HEAVENLY LIFE STRATEGIES

When we're growing in the Lord, we find many times that we allow other gods to creep into our lives—even after we become born again. Sometimes it takes years to feel like we're on the flip side of things. But you can fast forward quickly if you ask God to identify all the other gods in your life and all the things that you've put in higher priority than God—everything that is plugging up the open Heaven blessings. Then ask God to help rid your life of each and every one of those other gods.

If you want to be the change agent who is the portal for Heaven to come to earth, you need to be aware of what you are attracted to that is not of God. You need to know that when you're around those things or people or in those situations that you better activate some mental sanctification or the open Heaven blessings are not going to flow.

We have to be in love with our heavenly Father totally and completely in order to really experience the connection of open Heaven blessings. In Ephesians Paul speaks to the Church saying, *"Praise be to the God and Father of our Lord Jesus Christ, who has blessed us in the heavenly realms with every spiritual blessing in Christ"* (Eph. 1:3).

Later in that Scripture passage in Ephesians Paul says, in layman's terms, "Look, you've been chosen in Him before the foundation of the world. All these blessings are because you were predestined to be adopted as His children. You are to be the praise of the glory of His grace. You are accepted as His beloved. You are redeemed by His blood. You are forgiven of your sins according to the richness of His grace. You have all wisdom and prudence now. These are manifestations of the open Heaven coming upon you because they are spiritual blessings that are coming to you in the here and now. We can be open to all of these blessings. They are yours. All it takes is for you to look to Heaven and say, 'They are mine.'"

The following are a few strategies for how to live under an open Heaven. Aside from the fact that you have to ask God to show you about the other gods, you also have to speak, not only *speak* truth to yourself, but you have to *think* truth continually. In Philippians, we find this verse where it says, *"Rejoice in the Lord always. I will say it again: Rejoice! Let your gentleness be evident to all. The Lord is near. Do not be anxious about anything, but in every situation, by prayer and petition, with thanksgiving, present your requests to God"* (Phil 4:4-6). So, don't be anxious but with prayer and petition, with everything be thankful, present your request to God and what? *"And the peace of God, which transcends all understanding, will guard your hearts and your minds in Christ Jesus"* (Phil. 4:7).

And Paul also admonishes:

> *Finally, brothers and sisters, whatever is true, whatever is noble, whatever is right, whatever is pure, whatever is lovely, whatever is admirable—if anything is excellent or praiseworthy—think about such things. Whatever you have learned or received or heard from me, or seen in me—put it into practice. And the God of peace will be with you* (Philippians 4:8-9).

Why is that way of thinking so important? This is important because if you want to see and have open Heaven experiences, you have to be thinking as Heaven does: noble, right, pure, lovely, admirable, excellent, praiseworthy. That's how Heaven thinks all the time. Do you realize that Philippians 4:9 is a command? Many people brush right over that one and think, *Oh, yeah. I know I'm supposed to think right thoughts.* No, it's not a suggestion, it's a command. This means when you're thinking wrong thoughts, you need to immediately say to yourself, *No, I'm going to think right thoughts.* When you have mean thoughts about somebody, say to yourself, *No, I'm going to think about things that are admirable, true, noble, excellent.* Push negative thoughts quickly out of your mind.

When you change your thinking, Heaven is going to come into the situation right then and there, because you chose to obey the command and do what is right. When you don't, you lose. If you think, *Oh, yeah, whatever. I'm not thinking right things. So what?* Well, you just missed Heaven. That's what.

But don't be too hard on yourself, we all allow negative and wrong thoughts to invade our minds and linger there for too long. I'm not telling you anything that I don't have to brush up on myself. When I think things like that, I say to myself, *Wait a minute! The command says I'm supposed to be thinking excellent, noble, pure, right, and holy thoughts about this. I'm going to miss Heaven wanting to do something here unless I put this into action.* That's what needs to happen first.

Here's another thing. You need to ask God to show you your future. After you ask Him to sanctify your mind, ask Him to show your future. Think about it, the future could be a long time ahead of you. Or it can be the next minute of your life. All you have to do is ask Him to show you. You need to always walk in an expectation that you're living under Heaven. You need to be expecting Heaven to show up in this place—in you. There should be a level of expectation.

You need to create your own environment and stop allowing your environment to create you. When you live in open Heaven experiences, you have the right to create your own environment because Heaven has shown up on the scene. Instead of allowing the environment to create you while you shrink back thinking, *Well, Heaven might not show up because I'm in this environment*, let me tell you something, when you seek God, your faith will increase and He will change the environment and you'll see Heaven show up.

HEAVEN ARRIVED IN LAS VEGAS

Many years ago my husband and I went to Las Vegas with some of his friends from college and their wives and girlfriends. This was not a church planting time in my life—it was many years before that, just in case you're wondering.

Everyone was gambling and acting like they were having fun—that's what they were doing, acting. That setting is all a big illusion. Everybody is drinking, doing their own thing. I responded with this attitude, "Listen, this environment is going to change right now." Let me tell you, from the start I sat with women and ministered the Gospel to them. The guys my husband was with were surprised and started badgering him, "What's she doing? Doesn't she know where she is? She's not in church—this is a casino with gambling and alcohol. Why is she ministering the Gospel here?"

But the ladies were hurt and broken. They needed God. They were sick in their marriages. They were tired of their lives. They wanted peace. There was so much sin that they didn't know what to do. They were ready for Heaven to come to Las Vegas.

69

So I told the guys, "I don't care where I am. These people need this. So I'm going to minister." The men wanted me to stop but my husband said, "No, just leave her alone. Let her do what she needs to do."

We stayed there for about three nights. And every night I ministered—at the pool, at meals, wherever we were. I didn't care that I was on the streets of what many call "Sin City." No matter what we call it, God has many God-fearing ministries there trying to bring the Gospel to the streets. Sin City was going to have to bow to the power of the Holy Spirit. No matter where you are, you can still minister the Gospel. Las Vegas is in great need of our prayers and the spreading of the Gospel. Every city in our country and the world is in great need of our prayers and the Gospel. Just go to any street corner and you'll see.

Don't be afraid to present the gospel because of where you are. Even if you're in the worst environment you can possibly be, God has you there for a reason. If you're there for a reason, allow Heaven to open up upon you and be the portal. Be a portal of righteousness and holiness because God has you there for a reason. Decree His goodness and it shall be established and the light shall shine upon your ways.

When we cower down to sin and environments that aren't right, we aren't using what God put inside us to create a new environment. Every one of those women who went on that trip wanted to know the truth, God's truth. They wanted to know that there really was an answer. When they left that place, I know they thought to themselves, "My situation doesn't have to be like it is. I've got a choice. I can either change it or not change it." Too many people live in turmoil—they want change. They're not happy in Las Vegas or places that prey on human weaknesses. They're not happy. It's an illusion. It's all an illusion. It's all false. It's all counterfeit. It's all designed to get you to walk away from Heaven and worship something else.

Many environments are traps created by the enemy to coerce a need in you to be drawn to something that you didn't even know you thought you needed. It's manipulation. But you don't have to live as a manipulated individual. You can choose to change the situation.

Let me tell you what, if you have made that decision to change and reflect God's glory, everyone will want to be like you. I want you to say, "Everybody wants to be like me." They want to be like you because you had the guts to change the situation. But they may be too afraid of what somebody is going to say about them if they change.

Or is that you? If yes, stop being afraid of what somebody is going to say about you. If Jesus had been afraid about what others would say about Him, He wouldn't have died on the Cross for us. He wouldn't have gone there. He went to the Cross because He didn't care what they said about Him. They lied about Him and He said, "I know the truth and when I go, I will send the presence of the Holy Spirit. They will live in Heaven with Me even while they're on earth."

Ask now for God's forgiveness and look at the Cross. I know it's hard to look at Him, but His blood is what saves you. Look at Him and say, "Thank You, Jesus, that You loved me enough that I can start eternity right now on earth and be in heavenly encounters with You today."

I pray healing for you. I pray that you have the boldness to declare, decree, and establish His will for you so the Light can come upon you.

ENDNOTE

1. Drs. Adam and Cynthia Smithyman, *Soul Transformation: Your Personal Journey* (Nashville, TN: WestBowPress, 2015).

CHAPTER 5

HEAVENLY PILLAR

In our most recent chapter together, we learned that we can release Heaven on earth through declaring and decreeing the change God wants to make on earth. When we declare something, we're making declarations from Heaven about the things that God wants to see happen on the earth. That's different from confession. Confession is when we confess something on our heart that needs to be dealt with.

There's a big difference between confession and declaration. We confess in order to be authentic, so we can position ourselves to declare, so we can change our environments and our world. In order to be someone God positions to make declarations, you have to learn to confess authentically about what's going on in your life and around you. People who confess a lot are confessing about their current situations, confessing who they are apart from Christ.

These authentic confessions open a pathway for you to have power to be able to declare what needs to be said on earth from Heaven, because now you know who you are as a forgiven child of His and that He hears your prayers. *"If we confess our sins, he is faithful and just to forgive us our sins, and to cleanse us from all unrighteousness"* (1 John 1:9 KJV).

DECLARATIONS RELEASE HEAVEN

We want to become people who learn to release Heaven on the earth. Right? One way we do that is by learning how to make declarations. We pass through the confession stage and move to the declaration stage. To make a declaration means that you have to rise in your soul, your mind, your will, and emotions. In other words, you have to elevate your mental thinking to make a declaration.

It's very hard to make a declaration about anything, declaring something from Heaven, if you still feel like you're in the confession mode. You will not have the level of faith necessary to raise yourself to the position of being able to have the faith to declare a change. We have times in our lives when we need to confess to clean things out, but it's during that confession time that we don't feel like the most powerful people to want to declare something. We look at our lives and determine that we are not living right. We become law-focused and look at our behavior and lose our confidence to speak boldly. We don't see ourselves as Heaven sees us, which is the ability to rise and declare to bring change into the atmosphere.

Once when I was mentoring someone, she asked me to pray about a situation in her life. What she actually needed was for somebody to stand with her on it. When I prayed, I came from the immediate position of making declarations about what Heaven had said already about the situation and how we were going to stand in prayer for those things. At the end of the prayer time, she was astounded, saying, "Oh my gosh, I can totally see it, hear it, feel it, taste it. I can sense everything about it. It's going to happen." I responded in kind, further declaring, "Yes, it's going to happen. It's going to happen because you have positioned yourself to declare it, and we declared it over your life."

When it's a necessary time to declare, you can make a declaration from Heaven. You don't need to be concerned about whether or not you're good with God, because you *are* good with God because of what Jesus did. You can pray with confidence and come to the throne of grace to receive in your time of need because of what Jesus did on the Cross by shedding His blood. See what it says in Hebrews: *"Let us then approach God's throne of grace with confidence, so that we may receive mercy and find grace to help us in our time of need"* (Heb. 4:16). You don't have to be concerned about how you are going to pray into a situation, because we have God's Word to stand on. Don't pray from a place of doubt—pray from a place of faith.

When we connect with people who declare and decree, it means they've been to a place of rise. They have risen; they have elevated their thoughts to Heaven's perspective. They know who they are. They know where they stand. They know Jesus is interceding for them. They know what they say makes a difference. They know how to say what needs to be said because they know Heaven's perspective. They speak the Word and stand on the death, burial, and resurrection of Jesus as their access point to Heaven. Then the environment shifts. When you confess…confess to rise higher. Confess to position yourself to rise up so that you can begin to shift and start making declarations that are going to make a change. The rise or elevation begins first and foremost in your mind.

Remember how I mentioned I was going to go deeper into the story of Jacob in the next few chapters, well here is the last teaching in this chapter on him and the heavenly encounter he had in Bethel. In Genesis 28:10-22, we read about Jacob leaving Beersheba and setting out for Haran. Remember from the text, *"When he reached a certain place, he stopped for the night because the sun had set. Taking one of the stones there, he put it under his head and lay down to sleep"* (Gen. 28:11). So he makes a stone his pillow. What that stone represents is the fact that you can start anywhere in the process of your journey with God. There's always a starting point. The stone begins the journey.

YOUR STONE IS YOUR HEAVENLY STARTING POINT

The stone is not just a starting point, the stone also represents generations. Think about that for a minute. That stone had been in the dust. It had a history to it. Jacob lay his head down on a stone. Not only was it his moment in time when he was going to rest, but he chose to rest on something that had been around for generations. It had a past, and it was setting him up for his future.

After he lay his head on the stone, the Word tells us in Genesis 28:12 that Jacob had a dream. In this dream he saw a stairway resting on the earth, and as it was extended upward toward its summit, it reached to Heaven, and the angels of God were ascending and descending on it. In Jacob's dream, as his head was resting on this ancient stone, the Lord says to him, *"I am the Lord, the God of your father Abraham and the God of Isaac. I will give you and your descendants the land on which you are lying"* (Gen. 28:13). Jacob didn't even know that he stumbled in on this land that he and his descendants would inherit.

Now let's look at what else God says to Jacob in this encounter:

Your descendants will be like the dust of the earth, and you will spread out to the west, and to the east, to the north, and to the south. All peoples on earth will be blessed through you and your offspring. I am with you and will watch over you wherever you go, and I will bring you back to this land. I will not leave you until I have done what I have promised you (Genesis 28:14-15).

There's a lot to digest in that Scripture. Jacob's resting on his stone and enters into a dream state where a deposit of his destiny is surely coming.

GOD'S DREAM FOR US

Let's discuss a bit about how dreams are expressions of creativity. We're most creative when we are resting. We're least creative when we're bound, hurried, frustrated, quick, and moving fast. When we're resting, we position ourselves to receive from God so that He can speak to us the plans and purposes for our lives. Our night dreams become a place where God can deposit our destiny. Dreams, as in the realm or heart of creativity, also happen when we're not asleep; our eyes are open and we are resting, and we are believing God to speak to us in the same way as He did to Jacob, in a literal night dream. God talks to us all the time in the dreams and recesses of our hearts and in visions, thoughts, and ideas that He gives us. Where God deposits Himself in either our night dreams and or the recesses of our hearts, He is positioning us for our future.

Every dream that's developed has to go on through a journey. It's very interesting because God tells Jacob in Genesis 28:15 (I'm paraphrasing), "All these great things are a dream that's coming to you, Jacob. It's My desire for you. I'm going to deposit them inside you, but I want to tell you this, that I am with you always. I will watch over you wherever you go, and I will bring you back to this very space where you are right now. I'm not going to leave you until I've done what I have promised you." The dream had the stamp of God upon it. It had God's stamp of, "I'm going to be with you through the entire thing. I'm going to watch over you, and I'm going to provide for you until this thing is complete."

When God gives us a dream, the same is true for us. If God comes to you and He speaks to you about a plan and a purpose or even the future that He has for you, He intends to bring it to fruition; it will come to pass. He realizes it's going to be a long journey, and there's a past that's involved in it too. That's the whole essence of laying your head upon the stone. There's a past with it. There are generations before you, and there are generations in front of you as a result of what God is asking you to do.

And you know what's amazing? God will meet you in this heavenly place. The only thing He asks of us is to have faith, to have a heavenly mindset to follow after our God-given destiny. You see, your destiny is not earth-bound. It's a heavenly driven one that you carry out on the earth. Why is that an important statement? Let me tell you. It's important because declarations help take you from point A to point B when it comes to dreams.

SURELY, GOD IS IN THIS PLACE

God will always ask you to declare and decree things about yourself that He has said about you when you were on the journey process of Him developing dreams in you. He wants you to declare and believe with Him. When we make declarations, we're saying we've risen to a level of having the faith of God for the issue that's at hand, or for the destiny that's in hand. It's important that we declare and decree these things God says in the process.

When Jacob woke from his sleep, he thought, *"Surely the Lord is in this place, and I was not aware of it"* (Gen. 28:16). In other words, I laid my head on a stone. I had no consciousness, yet God showed up on the scene. When the dream came upon Jacob, all of a sudden he received a heavenly mindset. He became aware! Earthly mindsets live in the realm of the subconscious, always being urged to get their needs met; but people who live in the heavenly realm are always concerned about what God wants to do and how can they participate with Him to make that happen. Subconscious people are self-centered and self-focused. Heavenly minded people are for whatever God wants to do in the Kingdom and make declarations for Kingdom change.

God has to have you properly positioned at that place of rise or elevation in your mind. You have to come from rest to rise in order to be a mouthpiece to change whatever the Kingdom thing is that needs to be changed. We must be aware. Jacob was not aware until God came and uttered all of these things about his dream that quickened his spirit and his mind, which caused him to say, and I paraphrase, "I can start thinking about Heaven now. Heaven is here. Angels are descending and ascending. Surely God is in this place." When Heaven shows up, what do you say? "Whoa, surely God is in this place. I wasn't aware of it, but now I am aware."

It's very interesting that the Scripture says, *"Surely the Lord is in this place."* The root meaning in Hebrew of that word "place" quite literally and figuratively means the condition of the mind. The phrase "surely the Lord is in this place," according to the Hebrew, means surely the Lord is in our mind or our house. Surely the Lord is in the house inside of me. Surely the Lord is in my mind and in my heart and in my body. Surely the Lord is in this place—because your body is the temple of the Holy Spirit. You are the house of God.

Jacob came to recognize this in his own mind. When did he become aware of it? He became aware of the fact that Heaven said that God was in this place, which meant now, in this place of his mind. He agreed that in his house was his mind, and it could now shift and change and he could be what God called him to be. God spoke all that to him in the dream. When we're unaware, we cannot be the heavenly portal that God wants us to be. He has to make us aware.

Awareness comes when you first receive Jesus as your Lord and Savior; you get overwhelmed with the truth that you are completely and utterly forgiven of all of your sin by the God who loves you, who sent His precious Son to die and shed His blood for you, that you might be saved, redeemed, healed, transformed, and receive all the inheritance of Heaven. We receive this revelation initially, but the revelation grows as we mature. If you just stay there on that stone, you've missed the story. You'll never get to the Kingdom of God. You'll never get to the Kingdom of Heaven part, which is what He wants us to grab hold of so that we can live as Kingdom citizens on earth, fulfilling the assignment that God has given us. You can't fulfill the earthly assignment unless you understand the rules of the Kingdom and unless you understand heavenly rules.

After you become born again, the rest of your life is spent understanding what it's like to be a citizen of another world—while living here in the earthly realm. Why would God say, *"I am with you and will watch over you wherever you go, and I will bring you back to this land. I will not leave you until I have done what I have promised you"*

(Gen. 28:15)? Why would God say that? Because he knew that Jacob's mindset was not heavenly. He had a mindset that is unaware, that will doubt, question, and refute the dream. But God made it a point, in this time of Jacob's rest on the rock, to remind him that God will be with him wherever he goes, because Jacob's journey was going to be long. It was going to be so much harder than he could imagine before he would return to that place.

REST OPENS US TO HEAVEN

There's a key for heavenly encounters here. In the state of rest on that pillow is where God spoke to Jacob. It's in the state of rest that we position ourselves to have heavenly rest. Much like the Garden of Eden, there was rest in the garden. When we're resting, we're taking in the fullness and completeness of every element or provision that has been provided for us.

Let me ask you a question. When do you *not* rest in your heart, mind, and spirit? Answer: when you have worry, doubt, concern about provision, protection, or even acceptance. It's when you're wrestling in your subconscious about doubtful things.

However, when you really rest in the fact that you're complete in Him, totally, you will receive provision that comes from Heaven in union in Him. Then all of a sudden, you release into the heavenly realm a declaration about who you are and about what your situation is because you're full of faith and full of belief. When are you the fullest of faith and belief? When you know you're complete in Him, when you are totally and completely aware that He has made all provision for you. Then you decide you're going to have joy. Right? That's when you make the mental decision to say, "Okay, I think I'll be happy today. It looks like all the bills are paid and everything is good. I'm going to put on my happy face." It's all good. Right? No, tomorrow when trouble comes, I will freak out. But God says, "Listen, I'm with you all the way."

Right after Jacob proclaims, *"Surely God is in this place, and I was not aware of it"* (Genesis 28:16), then he says, *"How awesome is this place! This is none other than the house of God; this is the gate of heaven"* (Gen. 28:17). The gate of Heaven is where my purpose, my destiny, everything about who I am has been deposited into my spirit. By God, I have been made consciously aware of it. I know God is going to be with me. All provision is mine. He says He's going to carry me from here to there. Surely God is in this place!

PILLOW TO PILLAR

Do you hear my exclamation of celebration? The reality is, we celebrate when we have the fullness of all of these things. But do you have the fullness of all of these things? Yes! It was bought for you already. It's positioned for you already in the heavenly realms. You just have to rise to it. Now Jacob does a very interesting thing; after he hears all this, Scripture goes on to say, *"Early the next morning Jacob took the stone he had placed under his head* [as a place of rest] *and set it up as a pillar"* (Gen. 28:18). The stone went from being a pillow to a pillar. It went from a place of rest to a place of rise. Why? The man who was resting on it received from God the spark of energy because everything is complete now. He has all provision in God. Surely, God is in this place. Now, I'm going to make a pillar. I'm going to make a rise. I am elevated now. I'm going to make a statement.

As Jacob makes his statement, he takes the pillow, makes it a pillar, and he pours oil over it. He pours the fat portions of the greatest fruit so that all can see that this is richness, this is fullness, this is completeness, this is wholeness, this is going over that pillar. Then he names the place Bethel.

In this one passage of Scripture, everything changes; the man goes from rest to rise. I spoke of the significance of the pillar as an identity change in the last chapter. But in this one the emphasis is on rising or elevating. When you need a rise in your life, don't go down to the local bar; that's not your new identity in Christ any way. The world is not going to give you an elevation. People look for their rise in all the wrong places. The only right place is the place of rest in God, declaring and decreeing all that you have that Heaven says, and allow yourself to rest in that place until you rise in your mind, in your heart, in everything about yourself, and then you make a pillar that can be seen by everyone. You then become a monument of the Word that says, "When I declare and decree, change is made."

Bethel used to be called the city of Luz. Actually, in the Hebrew it means almond nut[1] or hazelnut. The almond tree is a symbol of the resurrection because it is the first to flower, was on the lampstand design in Exodus 25, and also on Aaron's rod that budded in Numbers 17. Jacob went from Luz, a place of resurrection, to Bethel, the house of God. In other words, he resurrected to the heavenly place in his soul. Isn't that incredibly powerful?

RISE TO POSITION

After Jacob set up the pillar, or monument, with his mouth he declares and makes a vow. There are five things that he says because he has a new identity now. He declares exactly what God said to him in a dream; but now, he's awake and has grasped his new identity. Jacob knows who he is. He has a heavenly mindset. He set up a pillar, and he tells anybody in the atmosphere who's listening, *"If God will be with me and will watch over me on this journey I am taking and will give me food to eat and clothes to wear so that I return safely to my father's household…"* (Gen. 28:20-21). Do you see that Jacob is stating his needs for provision and protection? He says, "I need God to be with me, and I need my food, clothes, safety, and want to go home." He then says, *"…then the Lord will be my God and this stone that I have set up as a pillar will be God's house, and of all that you give me I will give you a tenth"* (Gen. 28:21-22).

In other words, Jacob is making a declaration of everything that God has told him. He's saying it back to God, but now it's from the place of rise. He's saying it now from the place of a pillar instead of a pillow. He has positioned himself now, and, as he says it, he believes it. He has poured oil over this place. He's sure of who he is now—a man aware of all that God has for him. Then Jacob says he will give God a tenth or a tithe offering. He makes these declarations, and then determines to have one more action and that action is to give God an offering of a tenth of everything.

FAITH IN ACTION

Jacob offered God a tithe or a tenth of all the provision that God gave him. He called this stone God's house. Jacob was going to bring a tithe to the house of God continually. Not off of one moment, but as a constant. Bare minimum is tithing. But he says in his vow as he sets up the pillar, anoints it with oil, and claims all these things, he now says, *"of all that You give me I will surely give a tenth to You"* (Gen. 28:22 NASB). Every day God is blessing us, and every day we are to bless Him. In this passage, it is the tenth that is securing the faith in action.

Although I'm paraphrasing, in the simplest terms this is what he is saying, "God, I believe so much and I've done all this, but I'm going to do this other thing because I have so much faith that it's manifesting as an action." True repositioning requires an action. If you've truly risen, it requires action. If you've truly changed, it requires action. If you've truly gone to the place of resurrection and the answer is to do what God is asking you to do, that's the correct follow through. So as heavenly citizens, our job is to continually bless the King and honor the Lord with faith in action.

Take a look at what Hebrews says, *"But we are not those who shrink back to destruction, but of those who have faith to the preserving of the soul"* (Heb. 10:39 NASB). Make a pillar out of what God is speaking to you and in your new identity so that you encounter Heaven. Declare and decree what God has placed in your heart and this spiritual marker will be a reminder of the new position that God is giving you. Then walk out this heavenly call on earth through faith in action. This will continue to help you release Heaven on earth. Then make a lifestyle change as a risen person with a new identity to perpetually give, which means you now have perpetual access to Heaven.

Offerings unto God, as stated earlier in this chapter, will help position you with a right heart to create supernatural environments for heavenly encounters.

ENDNOTE

1. Almond; Bible Plants; Old Dominion University Plant SITE; http://ww2.odu.edu/~lmusselm/plant/bible/almond.php; accessed June 24, 2019.

PART II

HEAVENLY ENCOUNTERS THAT CREATE SUPERNATURAL ENVIRONMENTS

CHAPTER 6

CAUGHT UP TO HEAVEN

I would like to share with you my personal testimony of how I was caught up into the third heaven. It happened during the 2003-2004 time frame. My husband, Adam, and I were stationed at NAS Kingsville, in Kingsville, Texas. He was the executive officer at the naval air station, and we attended a wonderful church there—a multi ethnic, multicultural church. It was during that time when my husband really began to start walking in his spiritual giftings. During this time our pastor spoke to Adam that he had gifts also to pastor. My husband began to pray into this desire by stepping out and going to school and learning to pastor a church.

At this time I was busy with my radio and television ministry and was a Bible teacher and conference speaker. My heart was really for evangelism. I loved the church. I loved to teach in the church, but I wanted to get out and evangelize. My husband asked me if I would consider pastoring a church with him—to plant a church. I was very antagonistic toward that idea for a lot of different reasons. One of those reasons, just to be honest, was the fact that I was a female. I really wanted to do evangelism and I thought I wouldn't be well received if I was actually pastoring a church. That was a mental issue that I had to personally get over.

But that wasn't the total reason. I'm a free spirit. I love to travel to all kinds of places. My husband and I totally agree with that point about me. God has really had to train me in a lot of different areas, especially with pastoring. I absolutely love to pastor now, but it took a lot of years for that to happen.

During this time in our lives, my husband was away on a short military assignment, and I was at home. One day when our children were in school, I was worshipping the Lord, and was completely engrossed in a quiet time with Him. I'd been fasting and praying for about three days and was in about the middle of the fast. I had simply sat down to be in the presence of God. I just wanted to worship Him and get my thoughts straight and just focus.

TOTAL PEACE AND WHOLENESS

During that time, He literally caught me up to a different place where there was a lot of color, a lot of different colors. But it wasn't so much what I saw that completely transformed me. It wasn't like I walked out into some great field or opened a window or did anything of that sort, as are some people's testimonies of being caught up. It was simply that I was caught up to a place in the spirit where I had no sense of my own consciousness—no sense of consciousness at all. I was not even familiar with who I was as a person. Any weaknesses, insecurities, sin, anything earthly in my life was non-existent. I was completely and totally at one with God, in complete and total union with Him, a place where I could only recognize Him—not myself.

It was a place of complete wholeness and beauty and so completely overwhelming. I remember that I started to talk to the Lord and I saw a side of His face, but I didn't see His total face. I said, "Oh, I love it here. I don't want to go back. I don't want to go back." Here I was; I knew that I was married and that I loved my husband and I loved my children. But this place was so very wonderful that I didn't want to go back. I was so far gone from the earthly realm, in this place of total peace and utter wholeness. I was consumed by God and consumed by His presence.

I said to Him, "I do not want to go back," and He said, "You have to go back. You have to go back and tell the people what you've experienced. You have to go back."

"Oh my gosh, Lord, I don't want to." Then I was back in my body or at least as I can explain it, back into my own consciousness of self. I'm not sure if I was out of the body or in the body, just as Paul speaks of in Second Corinthians 12:2-4: *"I know a man...who was caught up to the third heaven."* Many believe Paul was speaking of himself. He said he didn't know whether he was *"in the body or out of the body."* He just knew that he was *"caught up to paradise,"* and I was as well in my heavenly encounter. When I came back to my conscience awareness, I immediately recognized that, "Oh! I'm me again. I'm me. I can feel me."

I had no consciousness of myself when I was with Him in that heavenly place. But when I came back, I had an instant consciousness of myself, and I just simply lay on the floor. I couldn't get up. It seemed like I was gone for hours, but when I looked at my watch, it was only about 45 minutes that I was gone. I just lay there and rested for a while, then I knew I had to get up because our children were coming home from school.

When they arrived, my oldest daughter, Alex, looked at me and said, "Oh, Mom, what happened to you? Something's happened to you. Where have you been? What's taking place?" I couldn't even talk.

She said, "You've encountered God. Something's happened." I was clearly in a daze and said, "Yes. Yes, I've had an experience, and I don't really want to talk about it right now."

Alex was very excited because she knew how much I loved the Lord, and I had been teaching the children about Him as well. My husband and I had been teaching them for years, so she was familiar with God.

I made them dinner, then said, "Let's get ready. It's almost time for church." When we arrived at church, I was really a wreck. I didn't put on any makeup that day, and all I wanted to do was to sit in the back of the church and not be bothered by anyone or anything. But Alex had gone to the pastor and said, "My mom had an experience… something happened to her and you need to go talk to her. You need to find out what's going on."

So the pastor came over to me and said, "Alex seems to think that something's happened to you. Are you all right?"

"Well, yes, I had an experience with God. It's so hard to explain, but I got caught up somewhere, and I had no consciousness of myself. It's even hard for me to talk right now. I really just want to sit."

He said, "No, you must talk. You need to come before the congregation and tell them what you experienced because these kinds of things are life-changing and will transform people's lives."

"Oh no, not today!" I just wanted to bask in His presence. But I went up to the front when the pastor called me shortly after he started the service. He said, "Candice, come up and share." The whole congregation was seated, and after I spoke only a few words, people started crying and weeping. I hadn't even shared the whole experience, but the glory of the Lord had dropped on all the people—they were experiencing God's presence so intently.

I began to cry. I cried because that's all I could do, even when I had come back from being in that place with Him. All I wanted to do was cry tears of joy as I was so touched by the Lord.

Then I could see that something had changed because the people were responding as though Heaven had touched them, literally touched them, because Heaven had touched me. I was deeply humbled.

FEED MY SHEEP

The next day I was still on my fast. I didn't want to eat. I had no appetite. I had been completely filled with my trip to Heaven, so I didn't even have a desire to eat. That day the Lord spoke to me. I heard Him loudly and clearly say to me three times, *Feed My sheep. Feed My sheep. Feed My sheep.* That phrase is in John chapter 21, when Jesus told Peter to feed His sheep.

I thought, *Oh my gosh. I've heard that before!* I went to the Word and looked it up. This is exactly when Jesus asked Peter to feed his sheep. *My God. You're asking me to feed Your sheep. You're asking me to pastor with my husband.* Immediately, I realized what He was saying and thought, *But Lord, that's not even fair. I mean, I don't wanted to do this at all, yet you took me to Heaven, and now You're asking me this. Of course, of course, I will do whatever You want me to do, Lord. When You take me into Your presence, yes, I will do whatever You want.*

93

My husband came home the next day and I told him about my experience. I said, "I now know I'm supposed to pastor a church with you. I'm now ready to plant a church." I believe God would get me ready in due time. It was shortly after that when we received orders to go to Chicago, and it was there we planted our very first church, Christ Cafe Church.

That's a whole other story of faith in and of itself—our first church was planted all on faith. We leaped out with no money, signed a lease on a 1,800-square-foot building, and simply started a church. We had a church planting consultant come and share with us how to plant a church, and we went and we did it. We sat under this consultant's leadership for a period of time.

Our church was filled with the glory of the Lord during every service and there were many healings and deliverances. People came from all over the Grayslake, Illinois, area to receive healing. We were even recognized by the *Chicago Tribune* newspaper as "the people who lived by crazy faith," in a few articles about us and our church plant. And of course, even still today, Freedom Destiny Church in Jacksonville, Florida, which is our second church plant, is the same way—full of faith, as you read in the first chapter of this book, and full of miraculous healings and deliverances.

I've had multiple experiences, multiple heavenly experiences. Since the time God took me to the third heaven and then said to me, "Feed My sheep," I have been pastoring and teaching and sharing the Word of God from an entirely different perspective. Because I have encountered Heaven, now what I read, see, and understand is totally from a heavenly perspective.

Knowing who I am in Christ and knowing that I am a glory portal for Heaven has made me realize that Heaven has come and deposited itself inside me. I know now that Heaven wants to be activated in supernatural environments through everyone who is ready and willing to receive.

I also want to mention that one of the things we need to keep in mind when we hear about people being caught up to Heaven or we hear about heavenly encounters is that heavenly encounters always produce something. They produce a benefit here on earth. Even for me, when I was caught up into that place. It was like Moses when he saw the burning bush, and he said, *"Here I am"* (Exod. 3:4). As a result of the dramatic heavenly encounter with the burning bush, Moses was changed. Then the Lord sent him out to deliver the people.

HEAVEN'S TOUCH

The same happened when Isaiah was touched with the coals and he said, *"Here am I. Send me!"* (Isa. 6:8) When Heaven comes and touches us, an action comes from it. God doesn't just catch us up to Heaven and expect us to do nothing. He expects that if we encounter Heaven, that by faith we will take action that will change our environments.

I've studied this subject a lot, and even after I've had my heavenly experiences, I always wanted an understanding and a confirmation of what happened to me through the Word of God. Consequently, God has shared a lot of His Word with me to help me communicate to others that when Heaven touches you, you are changed and transformed, and you must go out and do something as a result of it.

You do not experience heavenly encounters so you can sit around and boast. Even Paul agrees; he doesn't boast except in the Lord (see 2 Cor. 10:17). He even had a thorn in his flesh as a result of his heavenly encounter (2 Cor. 12:7). I have thorns in my flesh as a result of the heavenly encounters I've had, and I've just shared two of them. I have had multiple heavenly encounters and have seen amazing miracles happen. When I am in a place, things happen and things change, and I carry thorns and weights and have messengers, enemy messengers, that want to come and torment as a result of what I know about the heavenly realms.

However, they don't stop me, just like they didn't stop Paul, and they don't stop people who have been touched by Heaven. People who have truly been touched by Heaven keep going; they keep impacting their environments. They minister the Gospel and share with people the delight of knowing Jesus—knowing the fullness of Him, knowing His presence.

I say all this to encourage you. Yes, people do get caught up to Heaven. I was. I never physically died to access Heaven. I've talked to people with testimonies who have died and have seen so many marvels. Then they come back to life and share the reality of Heaven.

I've also talked to people who have been caught up like myself. One truth remains—in all heavenly encounters, people's lives were radically transformed and they wanted to serve God more and go out and make a difference for the Kingdom. Action to see Heaven change environments is one fruit that comes from encountering Heaven. You'll know if you've encountered Heaven because of the change that was made in your life after you returned from the encounter.

I say all this to share about being caught up to Heaven and how it still happens today. There are people who will say, "Oh, well, that just happened to Paul." Yes, that did happen to Paul—in the New Testament where he revealed it in Second Corinthians. We are part of the New Testament. We, the Ecclesia, the Church, are His body today. There are many believers who are living proof that being caught up is still happening today. You can ask, "God, I want to be caught up. I want to see You. I want to know You. I want to connect with You there." It is up to Him, of course, whether or not you encounter Him this way—but you can definitely ask.

God is looking for people with hearts who want to have heavenly encounters, who want to be connected with Him. He wants to reveal Himself, because when He reveals himself and your life has changed, you're going to go and bring Him to other people, and their lives are going to radically change. Fruit comes from truly encountering God and it manifests in your testimony that touches others with the love and grace of God. Nothing is impossible for God; if you sow to the Spirit, you will reap from the Spirit (see Gal. 6:8).

CHAPTER 7

HEAVENLY RICHES

There is a movie titled *Let There Be Light* that shares a story about what Heaven is like. I would like to share in my own words what the movie says about Heaven, because I feel it is so true. Heaven is kind of like this: There is a house with many rooms. And I am in my room, and you in your room. We are all in the same house but we are in different rooms. When I am in my room, I can't see you in your room, but we are still in the same house or same dimension.

You see, Heaven's just another room. You're that close to Heaven, now. It's just another room that you can't see at the moment. It's right next to you, but it's another room. And when people die, they just go to the other room; you can still be in the same house with them, and you can be cooking your meal or doing whatever. They've just gone to another room. It might take a lot of years for you to communicate with them again, but they are just in another room.

What do you think of that? I'm going to leave you with that thought.

Let's give thanks to God for His Son Jesus Christ who enabled us to go to Heaven and live in His house with many mansions. God wants to teach you the keys to eternal dwellings and how to manage the earthly realm, because a little management there opens the heavenly dwellings and the riches here.

In this chapter you are going to encounter a word about heavenly riches and more importantly, how to *manage* heavenly riches. I know you might say and may even be thinking, *Well, you know what, Pastor Candice, why are you trying to teach me about heavenly riches? I'm just trying to manage what I've got in my hand right now. I see heavenly riches as something that's too far-fetched. I don't think I can grab hold of this teaching because what's in my hand doesn't seem heavenly at all.* I want to talk to you about how to change your mindset about Heaven's riches. Let me tell you, this is going to break down some walls. It's going to reposition you to understand how God's economy works.

We know from Psalm 50:9-12 that our Lord has no need of anything, right? The Lord says:

> *I have no need of a bull from your stall or of goats from your pens, for every animal of the forest is mine, and the cattle on a thousand hills. I know every bird in the mountains, and the insects in the fields are mine. If I were hungry I would not tell you, for the world is Mine, and all that is in it* (Psalm 50:9-12).

Is that not powerful? God is saying, "This is who I am, and this is what I have, so why would I bother telling you what I need. I already own it all!" The Word of God is a heavenly word. It was given to humankind through the inspiration of God because it "...

penetrates even to dividing soul and spirit, joints and marrow; it judges the thoughts and attitudes of the heart" (Heb. 4:12). This is the truth of Heaven. So, we're going to understand our God. He owns all riches. Therefore, we're going to discuss how God owning everything affects how we think.

ETERNAL DWELLINGS ARE OPENING

Jesus says in Matthew 6:24, *"No one can serve two masters. Either you will hate the one and love the other, or you will be devoted to the one and despise the other. You cannot serve both God and money."* The Pharisees who loved money heard all this and they were sneering at Jesus. But He said to them, *"You are the ones who justify yourselves in the eyes of others, but God knows your hearts"* (Luke 16:15). What people highly value is detestable in God's sight. Change your thinking. What you have in your hand is worldly wealth. That's all that it is. It operates in this realm. That's all that it does. When you choose to give it away, you open for yourself eternal dwellings that bring down the "much" from Heaven for you to occupy and for you to manage.

Are you getting this?

What you have in your hand is little, according to Heaven. It's practically nothing. You may have thought it had a lot of value and you want to hold on to it. I know you're concerned about it. I know that you wonder what you're supposed to do with it.

Giving to others, even what you do not own, will open eternal dwellings of Heaven, and then you enter into a place where who takes care of you? Heaven, God, the One who owns everything and doesn't need what you have. This is a principle of giving that opens the Heavens to release heavenly riches. You see, God owns it all. If God is saying He's teaching us now how to operate in the heavenly realms of riches, we have to understand what's important to God is how we manage the little, which is what the earth has given us. If you're not managing this right, you're not going to be able to manage Heaven's wealth. Why? Because Heaven's riches you can't even see, as He owns it all. He sends it to the ones He knows can manage well.

You're only managing well if you're a giver. You're only managing well if you position yourself into the other realm and determine, "I don't need any of this. He owns it all. I want what Heaven has more than what this place has. I'm going to give away what I need to give away in accordance with what God says to give away; because when I open myself up to receive Heaven's riches, instead of burying myself in the riches of this world, that's what will be truly valued in light of eternity."

MANAGING THE LITTLE

This spiritual insight is really powerful—if you can wrap your head around this, you will stop being concerned about what you have and what you owe because where's your true wealth? Is it in your pocket or the bank? No. I don't even care if you are a billionaire. It doesn't make a bit of difference. That's worldly wealth. God owns more than dollars and cents. He owns the earth we stand on. Now, if He says, "I own everything. " Then what He's saying is, "I'm a dad who just wants to give to you."

When you understand heavenly riches on earth and begin to operate in the "much," which is the heavenly much, it means that by faith, when you look at your worldly wealth, you do not give it too much value because Heaven doesn't give it much value; God calls it the little. He doesn't call it the much. He says the much isn't there. So when you can manage this right by giving it away and not being fearful of where it's going or whether or not you're going to eat, and you stop being trapped in what you have, He'll respond in kind and say, "Listen, if I own all things and you're My kid, I'm not going to allow you to be in need."

He's not going to do that. No good dad would ever do that. You can't call God a good God if that were the case. Not only does He own everything in Heaven and earth, He owns you too. He owns your breath. He owns everything about you. So, you have to learn how to manage earthly wealth as though it were a little—that's what makes you worthy of managing heavenly riches.

We cry out to God all the time about wanting to tap into Heaven, to see Heaven, to be part of Heaven, to walk in Heaven on earth, to walk in the glory. If that's your heart's cry to God and you're really praying those prayers, then one of the tests He has for you is how you manage your worldly wealth; because He calls it little.

Before we discuss a principle related to Deuteronomy 8, let's go to the Parable of the Shrewd Manager in Luke 16:8-13 in the Amplified Bible to confirm that what I'm sharing with you about heavenly riches is from the Bible:

> *And his master commended the unjust manager [not for his misdeeds, but] because he had acted shrewdly [by preparing for his future unemployment]; for the sons of this age [the non-believers] are shrewder in relation to their own kind [that is, to the ways of the secular world] than are the sons of light [the believers]. And I tell you [learn from this], make friends for yourselves [for eternity] by means of the wealth of unrighteousness [that is, use material resources as a way to further the work of God],*

so that when it runs out, they will welcome you into the eternal dwellings.

He who is faithful in a very little thing is also faithful in much; and he who is dishonest in a very little thing is also dishonest in much. Therefore if you have not been faithful in **the use of earthly wealth, who will entrust the true riches to you?** *And* **if you have not been faithful in the use of that [earthly wealth] which belongs to another [whether God or man, and of which you are a trustee], who will give you that which is your own?** *No servant can serve two masters; for either he will hate the one and love the other, or he will stand devotedly by the one and despise the other.* **You cannot serve both God and mammon [that is, your earthly possessions or anything else you trust in and rely on instead of God].**

The Amplified Bible expands the text to offer a bit more insight. The manager prepared for his future unemployment. He knew he was not going to have any money. Nonbelievers are shrewd. They understand how to operate in the secular world of wealth.

In other words, nonbelievers are even giving as they are cutting debts or giving money away in order to save their own skin. Why? Because they know that's all they have, so they're trying to figure out a way to live. We, as believers, shouldn't be concerned about that, as we are sons and daughters and our Father provides all things. If you don't know the Father, then you would have to operate from a worldly standpoint. So, as the sons and daughters of the light, as believers, He's saying, "Listen, even nonbelievers have it figured out more than believers do."

You will make friends for yourselves for eternity by means of spreading the worldly wealth of man. If you are using your material resources to further the work of God, then when it runs out, all of these worldly, temporal folks will welcome you into eternal dwellings.

In other words, the people that you end up giving to, or that you end up blessing for the Kingdom of God opens up for you eternal gateways in the heavens where you're able to access Heaven's resources because you've made the choice to do that.

When I pondered these Scriptures, I thought to myself, You mean to tell me that when we give to churches, charities, any organizations, or just individuals in need, these people hold our eternal dwelling and our opportunity to step into heavenly riches? Yes, these people hold your access to heavenly eternal dwellings. Now that's huge, because that means giving to them will open a heavenly door. God says they hold the key to the eternal dwellings, eternal habitations, and the blessings of the Kingdom of Heaven for you. Why would God say that? Because we're believers and we should be thinking at a higher level than the nonbeliever, right? We should be thinking about Heaven on a continual basis. And so, it's important for us to remember this.

EVERY WORD FROM GOD

Now, let's go to Deuteronomy chapter 8; all these Scriptures tie into this.

When the Israelites were crossing the desert, they were told:

> *Be careful to follow every command I am giving you today, so that you may live and increase and may enter and possess the land the Lord promised on oath to your*

ancestors. Remember how the Lord your God led you all the way into the wilderness these forty years..." (Deuteronomy 8:1-2).

To what? Why the desert?

...to humble you and test you in order to know what was in your heart, whether or not you would keep his commands. He humbled you, causing you to hunger and then feeding you with manna, which neither you nor your ancestors had known, to teach you that man does not live on bread alone but on every word that comes from the mouth of the Lord. Your clothes did not wear out and your feet did not swell during these forty years (Deuteronomy 8:2-4).

Manna was a food that came down from Heaven as nourishment for the journeying Israelites. It dropped every day and the people were given a command by God to pick up only what was necessary for that day. If they disobeyed God and put more in their pocket, what happened to it? It became infested with maggots and rotted. God was not pleased. Why would someone take more, when God drops it from Heaven? Why would anybody take more? They take more because they don't believe they're going to get it tomorrow, because they don't believe Him. Right? Or they're greedy. What drives greed? Fear.

Now listen, where I'm going with this is, if you want to tap into heavenly riches, you're actually tapping into a place where you're living on earth *"...on every word that comes from the mouth of the Lord"* (Deut. 8:3). That's the strategy for having Heaven's resources deposited to you. The Word says that He humbled the people and tested them with the manna in the wilderness to do what? To show them what? That people do not leave by bread alone, but by every word that comes out of the mouth of the Lord. In other words, He was training them to follow the commands that He had given them, which was to do this or don't do that.

He knew they needed to eat, so He sent it straight down from Heaven, it was a direct-from-Heaven blessing. But instead of believing there would be enough for them again tomorrow, they would take too much for themselves today.

Did you understand what I'm saying? If you tap into the heavenly realm, you might have zero in your checkbook, but you know that you will still eat the next day. Right?

God wants us to enter a heavenly place on earth where we have no fear. He doesn't want you to live by fear because people who have fear are greedy. They do crazy things. So, the strategy to tap into heavenly riches is to make sure that you live by every word that proceeds from the mouth of the Lord, which means when you wake up in the morning, you say, "What's the strategy for today, God? I don't know where I'm eating. I don't know how I'm paying my bills. But I do know who's taking care of me today—You, God! Show me what I'm supposed to do. I have this much, show me who to give it to. Show me, Lord Jesus, what the plan is for today. I don't want to be in fear. I am taking what You give me from Heaven and I am not fearful that You won't give it to me tomorrow. I release it today knowing that You will provide for me tomorrow as you did yesterday and will today. Thank You, Lord!"

In Heaven there is no fear. If Heaven is coming to earth, there should be no fear here. So when God says to manage heavenly riches, He's saying that you have to get to a place in your financial situation where you don't live by fear—you live by believing that your giving opens eternal habitations or dwellings for you. Then you are positioned for a place in Heaven where that resource will come down to you simply because it's good. Because He owns all the cattle on a thousand hills.

I hope you understand what I'm saying. What's important to God is that we learn how to manage heavenly resources. He doesn't care about the earthly, which He calls the little, but too many people in the earthly realm are mismanaging what God has actually allowed them to manage. And they are mismanaging by not giving! I'm paraphrasing here, but this is what He is saying, "I can't give them Heaven because they can't even manage earth right. Managing earth right means not being scared to death to give away what's in their pocket. Being scared to death is not Kingdom or heavenly living. They hold on to their earthly wealth like it's the only manna I'm ever going to give them."

We cannot be the Church of Jesus Christ, living in Heaven on earth, until we learn to stop living by fear in our financial situation and we begin to tap into our heavenly riches, which indeed are endless. God sees from Heaven that we gave it. It does not matter what they do with it or who received it. This is about your heart. When you have a heart to give, you're okay with God.

He tells us in a passage in Matthew, *"Do not store up for yourself treasures on earth, where moths and vermin destroy..."* (Matt. 6:19). In other words, if you're greedy, it's going to be gone out of your hands faster than you can imagine. Holding on opens you up not to eternal dwellings but to moths and vermin to come in and destroy. *"But store for yourselves treasures in heaven, where moths and vermin do not destroy, and where thieves do not break in and steal. For where your treasure is, there your heart will be also"* (Matt. 6:20-21). Where is your treasure?

Is it in your earthly little things? Is it in your house, your cars, your whatevers? Is that where it is, or is it in your treasure in Heaven?

PROMOTION TO HEAVENLY RICHES

There are mansions in Heaven; that is what Jesus says in John 14:2. There are things in Heaven that God has set aside for you; and when you begin to learn to give right without fear, it opens the highways and the byways of Heaven to give to you the heavenly thing that He wants you to manage. Come on, really think about it for a second. There's something on earth that God has assigned to you to manage from Heaven, and the test is: Are you going to position yourself properly to be a person who becomes a giver, instead of a getter? Where can you begin to position yourself to receive?

God has something for each one of us. He knows what you need. He knows you're crying out for Heaven, and He knows you're crying out for the resources and the riches of Heaven. He wants you to be there because He wants to see Heaven activated on earth. He wants to see that!

But the test is to stop looking at it as if it is bigger than what it really is to God. We must have His perspective, knowing that earthly wealth is little. The management of the earth is little. The management of Heaven is great. God says, "I'm looking for stewards who have established these principles in their hearts, in which case I can open the floodgates of Heaven and pour out a blessing that they have never seen before, because in that, I am trusting you." God is saying He trusts the one with the heavenly riches. Are you the one with the heavenly riches?

If you're a giver, if you're somebody who says, "I'm not going to be afraid. What's here belongs to You, God. I'm not going to hold on to it more than I need to. God, I'm going to live by every word that proceeds from Your mouth today. If you say, 'Do this,' I'm going to do it, and then I know that I'm going to step into the provision of having, because I made a choice in the earthly realm to listen to what You say, and to do what You have told me to do." Then you are living as a heavenly citizen on earth and you are activating the treasures of Heaven to be released to the earth. You are a manager of the BIG! You are a manager of heavenly riches.

In this chapter, you were taught a strategy. Humanity does not live by bread alone but by every word that proceeds out of the mouth of the Lord. God's training His Church and He is going to come back. He's going to rule and reign. And we are called to be Kingdom expanders who don't wait for Him to return to rule and reign—we do it now by allowing Heaven to come to earth, and deciding not to allow fear to cripple us.

God is testing to see if you believe in the earthly realm and the here and now more than what is said about Heaven. God wants to know if you're willing to work out your faith with fear and trembling, and do what He is telling you to do. Then you will truly begin to release Heaven on earth.

When you begin to exercise your authority and understanding on how to release Heaven into the atmosphere, you're not only going to tap into financial blessing, you're going to tap into the blessings that your spirit is crying out for including:

- the presence of God
- walking in greater gifts
- seeing healings and deliverances

- speaking with authority and giving a word of life into someone
- seeing people being resurrected from the dead

That is what being Heaven on earth is all about. That's what you are praying for, and that's what He says He's going to bring even more of—heavenly riches. Finances are not a problem for the Lord. He has no problems. He is trying to train us to believe He is with us and He provides!

CHAPTER 8

ACCESSING HEAVENLY TREASURIES

There have been many times when I have had visions given to me by the Holy Spirit that included a royal palace in Heaven. I have only seen one, but we know there are many mansions in Heaven because Jesus tells us this in John 14:2 (KJV): *"In my Father's house are many mansions: if it were not so, I would have told you. I go to prepare a place for you."*

At the royal palace I saw the royal banquet table spoken of in Isaiah 25:6: *"On this mountain the Lord Almighty will prepare a feast of rich food for all peoples, a banquet of aged wine—the best of meats and the finest of wines."*

It is a very long table with golden lampstands that burn the oil of the vats of Heaven. There is also oil on the table in a golden bowl and each person has one; you can put it on your hands or dip your bread in it. The bread is on the table that represents His revelation. There is wine in golden chalices at the table. The plates are golden and so are the eating utensils. There is some silver on the table, but it is almost entirely gold. The fruit is huge, and there are lots of grapes.

I saw Jesus sitting at the head of the table wearing a crown. He loves to smile and enjoys the food and the people. When He talks or laughs, the glory of the Lord comes forth strong like in a word to us. He also likes to hug us at the table and to hold our hands. He accepts everyone at the table because they are in attendance not based on their performance—they are there based on His performance, His sacrifice, and the access He gave them.

I have also seen the heavenly vats in these visions. I did not know they existed until I read about them in Hosea 2. They are located on the top floor of this palace I was in. I had to walk up some small hidden steps to get to them. There is the vat of wine which represents opportunity. There is a vat of oil which is the anointing oil of Heaven. There is a vat of gold which is full of gold coins. There is also a vat filled with grain which is the revelation of Heaven.

Anytime someone is in need on earth, they can go to the vats in Heaven and grab what they need and it will come from Heaven for them. They are to walk up to the heavenly vats and stand on the ladder that is there and stick their hand in and grab what is needed. Sometimes the vats actually overflow and come down into the earthly realm. But we have access to them now; we don't have to wait.

There is a royal suite with a midnight blue bedspread on a bed with mahogany bedposts. The bedspread has a gold fringe and gold designs embroidered on it, although I couldn't make out what the design was. It felt like velvet when I touched it. There was a smaller room off the royal suite that led to an underground area where I saw armies and horses. It was all very regal and quite magnificent to admire. But remember, the earthly realm is only a pattern of the heavenly realm; do not think that what you see here in the earthly realm came first. On the contrary, this came second, after Heaven. Every idea we have here was first thought by God and resided in Heaven. It is then transferred into our thoughts and minds.

There was another room on the left side of the palace that was filled with every kind jewel imaginable, as well as treasure chests absolutely overflowing with jewels. Imagine that for a second—but now also realize that we have access to all those jewels! All the things in Heaven are made in an instant, they do not need the same elements and processes as needed on earth. Everything we have on earth was first produced in Heaven—and we have been given access. The problem is, we don't take advantage of the access we have. We act like we don't have it because we don't exercise our rights as citizens of Heaven. This is what I've learned during my heavenly visitations with the Lord.

TREASURIES IN HEAVEN

Now I am going to share with you Scriptures about the treasuries in Heaven to give you a more in-depth perspective into how you can personally access them. I pray God gives you supernatural understanding so you can tap into this by faith and begin to see the treasuries in Heaven and access them. I am believing the seed of the Word of God in this chapter will create a desire in you to know more about heavenly blessings and how to access them in the earthly realm. You do not have to wait until you pass away in order to receive heavenly blessings.

While Jesus walked on earth, He had access to Heaven the entire time! And now, because we have the Holy Spirit within us, He gives us the authority and the power to walk just as He did. People often think that Jesus did it but they can't. But He came as an example for us. When Jesus died on the Cross, He bought for us the inheritance of Heaven. We can enjoy that access freely right now, it is not something we enjoy only after we pass from this world into Heaven. This is very important to understand because a lot of people theologically think that the blessings of Heaven are only available to you when you die in the earthly realm, when your spirit goes to Heaven. But that is not the truth.

The curses of the earth went on the Cross with Jesus. The curses died and were buried with Jesus. Three days later Jesus was resurrected—but the curses still remained dead and buried. Those curses prevented us from accessing the heavenly realm, but we are now free to walk in the power and blessings of Heaven in the here and now. Jesus took away all of the boundaries and obstacles from us. Jesus walked in the fullness of Heaven on earth—now we can too.

TREASURY GIFTS

God gives us gifts from the heavenly treasury—we have access to those gifts, but we have to open our hearts and minds to learn and understand. These truths are going to shake you, but they're also going to change you.

In the treasuries of Heaven, there is new grain, new wine, new oil, gold, and there is time. These are commodities we ask God for every day. You may not even realize that you're asking God for these things, but you are. You're asking God to give you a strategy, or a word from Heaven. You're asking Him for new wine when you say, I want a new position, I want to occupy, and I want to have joy! I want to step into these things that You've given me. When you ask for oil, you're asking for His anointing, you're asking for His power on your life. When you ask Him for gold, you're asking for the resources to do and have the provision for the vision that God has given you. Time always seems to be slipping away; it is a resource we are in desperate need of. We want to know how quickly we can take care of everything that needs to be taken care of so we can give Him glory and honor.

You may have personal dreams and visions and covenants that you've made with God throughout your past that have not come to pass yet. You might have even forgotten about them, but God wants you to call those things forth from Heaven into the earthly realm. We are told that God *"calls into being things that were not"* (Rom. 4:17)—and we can too. Just as Abraham and Sarah had to do their part when God spoke to them and said, *"I will surely bless you and make your descendants as numerous as the stars in the sky and as the sand on the seashore..."* (Gen. 22:17). Abraham had to trust God for that when he had no children at all at that time. Therefore, when God says something to us and we don't see it right away, we often bury it, not trusting His Word or His timing. However, our God is an everlasting God; and you must realize that you exist now, and you also exist in eternity at this exact moment in time.

Time and space are within an eternal time frame. Believe it! It's an everlasting time frame. But we as earthly creatures often don't look at time and eternity from this perspective. The apostle Paul even tells us this in Second Corinthians 4:18, *"So we fix our eyes not on what is seen, but on what is unseen, since what is seen is temporary, but what is unseen is eternal."*

We view things from a temporal and earthy perspective. We think, *Okay, well, maybe I've got so many years on this planet. My days are numbered.* Yes, that is true, our days are numbered and the Word does say that (see Ps. 90:12). However, your days of *existence* are never numbered. If this is all the existence that you have, then yes, your days are numbered—but it's not. It's not because you'll live forever. You will live forever and so time is a resource, a commodity, a blessing from Heaven that we have to learn to tap into from our temporal existence here on earth.

Let's look at Deuteronomy 28:12-14 again, this time from the King James Version:

> ***The Lord shall open unto thee his good treasure****, the heaven to give the rain unto thy land in his season, and to bless all the work of thine hand: and thou shalt lend unto many nations, and thou shalt not borrow. And the Lord shall make thee the head, and not the tail; and thou shalt be above only, and thou shalt not be beneath;* **if that thou hearken unto the commandments of the Lord thy God, which I command thee this day, to observe and to do them: And thou shalt not go aside from any of the words which I command thee this day***, to the right hand, or to the left, to go after other gods to serve them.*

ACCESS HEAVENLY TREASURIES
BY FAITH AND WORD

God is telling us how we get our blessings, but He also says there are treasuries. He has a good treasure for us. Now, how does this treasure come about? Well, it comes about when we obey His commands. When we position ourselves to know His Word, respond to His words, speak to His Word. His Word is what gives us access to the treasuries. His blood gave us access. You cannot go to the throne without death, burial, and resurrection in Christ. Although He died, when you believe in Him, you die too. This is what the Word says,

"For if we have been united with him in a death like his, we will certainly also be united with him in a resurrection like his" (Rom. 6:5).

So, you have access to the treasure. The question is whether or not you will accept the access. The Word gives you access because the written Word, when we obey it, positions us to be able to open the treasuries and bring them forth. You can't access the treasury if you don't believe it is there. You have to first believe it is there by faith! God says there is treasure in His Word. He says that in Matthew 6:19-20. We don't question what He says, right? He said there's a treasure and the Word is a key to open that treasure chest. So, the first thing that you have to understand about accessing the treasures of Heaven is that there is a treasure chest with multiple gifts for you.

These gifts are not based on your performance. These gifts are not based on whether or not you had an A day or an F day, if it was a good hair day or a bad hair day. It does not matter. The treasures are yours. Now why is that? Because you did not pay the price for those treasures. They are gifts from the One who paid the price and took the curse so that you may have access to them in the here and now. The foundation stone to accessing heavenly treasures is knowing there is a treasury and Jesus gave you access to it—and knowing that the Word opens this treasury.

THE FIRST KEY TO ACCESSING HEAVENLY TREASURES

The first key is knowing there are actually treasures in Heaven for you. This Word is found in Matthew 6:19-21 (NASB):

> *Do not store up for yourselves treasures on earth, where moth and rust destroy, and where thieves break in and steal. But store up for yourselves treasures in heaven,*

where neither moth nor rust destroys, and where thieves do not break in or steal; for where your treasure is, there your heart will be also.

When some people read that Scripture, they determine that they are developing treasures while here on earth for a numbered set of days. Even more so, they do certain things or respond certain ways, and by doing so they believe there will be treasures in Heaven they can access when they get there. But guess what? You are timeless. You are an eternal creature *now*. If not, why would this particular Scripture say to *"store up for yourselves treasures in heaven…For where your treasure is, there your heart will be also"*?

I need you to think differently because the treasury is there and He says specifically that where your heart is, your treasure is going to be. We have come to the logical place of understanding that earthly treasures we will leave here when we go to be with Jesus in Heaven. Right? We have believed that and understand that from the logical realm. The Word says, *"For where your treasure is, there your heart will be also"* (Matt. 6:21). "Treasure is" means it's happening now. Where your treasure is, that's where your heart is going to be. It is operating now. It is an eternal truth coming to a temporal realm. It's not that you have to wait for your treasure when your body dies. Your treasure is now!

If I have a treasure in the now but can't access it, I'm going to get a little frustrated. "Where is my stuff? I want this treasure. You say that you have this for me. Well, where is it? I believe it is there, God. So, where is this treasure?"

The following is a here and now word that will position you to access your current treasure.

Remember, you're timeless. Everlasting life is what you have. When you have everlasting life, it is for now because in the now is the everlasting. A treasure needs a treasury or a depository, an armory, a cellar; it needs a store-up place. God has huge treasuries available. He wants to give them to His kids, but His kids put all their thoughts on what's happening right now on earth. His kids are temporal thinkers, they think earthly first. You're going to be trained how to think eternally, not temporally.

We teach our children to think temporally. What would happen to your family if you began to teach your kids from day one that they're eternal beings? They're eternal and have a choice to live in Heaven or go to hell, but either way they will live eternally.

However, by knowing Jesus Christ as their Lord and Savior, they will live eternally with Him, and they also have a current power in the Holy Spirit that goes beyond the temporal. What would happen to your family if you began to teach them from the beginning that they are eternal and have access to the eternal treasuries of Heaven in the here and now? How would your family life and relationships change if you taught them that while they are in a current temporal state, while they are in this earthly realm, they also have access to the eternal treasures of Heaven—that they do not have to wait until they pass away.

At the very beginning stages of life our young have a "lack" mindset and this positions them for a life of fear. It's true that many people live in daily fear. Where does that come from? Adam and Eve, right? We were born into lack. We didn't have to be taught it, we were born with it already as part of our souls, minds, wills, and emotions. But Jesus bought abundance with Him and destroyed our lack—if we accept Him as our Lord and Savior, the Son of God. It's up to us; we have to change our thinking.

THE SECOND KEY TO ACCESSING HEAVENLY TREASURES

Now you are ready for the second key to accessing the heavenly treasuries: *You have to know that you're royalty in order to access the treasures.*

I'm sorry, but peasants don't receive the treasures. The king's children get the treasures because the king's children are the sons and the daughters. Now, how do I know this? Matthew 17:24-27 says:

> *After Jesus and his disciples arrived in Capernaum, the collectors of the two-drachma temple tax came to Peter and asked, "Doesn't your teacher pay the temple tax?"*
>
> *"Yes, he does," he replied.*
>
> *When Peter came into the house, Jesus was the first to speak. "What do you think, Simon?" he asked. "From whom do the kings of the earth collect duty and taxes—from their own children or from others?"*
>
> *"From others," Peter answered.*
>
> *"Then the children are exempt," Jesus said to him. "But so that we may not cause offense, go to the lake and throw out your line. Take the first fish you catch; open its mouth and you will find a four-drachma coin. Take it and give it to them for my tax and yours."*

In other words, this is a conversation about earth and Heaven. Simon Peter is saying, "Listen, Jesus, they're coming to ask for this tax." And Jesus doesn't say yes or no to the tax, but instead throws the question back to Simon Peter; He wants to teach him something. Jesus, in essence, asks, "Who are they coming for? The children or others? They're asking Me for the tax money, but guess what? The children are exempt. Simon Peter, you don't know who you are yet, you are a son and you are exempt from this tax." Yet the Word tells us that Jesus says so not to offend, *"go to the lake and throw out your line. Take the first fish you catch; open its mouth and you will find a four-drachma coin. Take it and give it to them for my tax and yours"* (Matt. 17:27).

So, in other words, Jesus is saying, "Simon Peter, you and I are sons. We're exempt; but because the earth is requiring a tax, guess where I'm going to get the money? I'm going to access the heavenly treasuries to get it, and I'm going to send you into the water to find a fish that will have exactly what we need in its mouth." Now, where did the fish get the money?

Remember that Word says there are treasures in Heaven: *"Do not store up for yourselves treasures on earth.... But store up for yourselves treasures in heaven.... For where your treasure is, there your heart will be also"* (Matt. 6:19-21). We are hearing Him, right? Jesus tells Simon Peter to go get the money from Heaven. So, Simon Peter goes and gets it. And now today, God's telling His sons and daughters to go and access their heavenly treasures. Like Simon Peter retrieved the treasure, we are to retrieve ours as well.

THE THIRD HEAVENLY KEY TO ACCESSING HEAVENLY TREASURES

Okay, now you are ready for *the third heavenly key—the key of time.* Galatians says:

Do not be deceived. God cannot be mocked. A man reaps what he sows. Whoever sows to please their flesh, from the flesh will reap destruction; whoever sows to please the Spirit, from the Spirit will reap eternal life (Galatians 6:7-8).

The flesh is earthly. The Spirit is everlasting, it is eternal. The flesh is temporal, but the Spirit is eternal. So, here the Word is saying if we want to reap from the heavenly treasures, we have to start sowing God's Word into our spirit, not to the flesh.

If you keep feeding the flesh, thinking that you don't have enough of this or that, thinking time is running out, and focusing on the fear, then you are not positioning yourself to sow into your spirit the treasures of God. You won't have the energy to tap into the everlasting life that's been given to you.

A heavenly key to access the heavenly treasury is knowing that it's everlasting, the treasure is always there. God's treasuries keep producing—they never stop producing. Earthly treasuries run out when it's all spent, but heavenly treasuries are always being poured out. There are continual reserves that never run dry.

So, we have to sow properly into our spirit. What is sown into the spirit? God's Word is to be sown into your spirit and your soul. You read the Word and then speak the Word and then you will believe you are eternal and not temporal. Eternal people know how to access things that are eternal. You're changing your destination now by believing the Word of God. You must stop thinking that destination is only accessible when you die. The destination is now, but it's also your future. Destination comes from the word "destiny." So, you need to begin to change how you think about sowing into your spirit. You need to sow into everlasting life with the Word of God.

TIME—AN EVERLASTING COMMODITY

Everlasting life is eternal. It's past, present, and future. It is a commodity. It is part of the treasuries. Why would time be part of the treasuries? Let me tell you why. This is obvious, because what do you fear the most when it's gone? Time. What creates anxiety in your life? Time. When we view time from an earthly perspective, there is a lot to fear because time passes so easily and quickly. We seem to never have enough of it. There's never enough time to spend with our kids or our spouse. There's never enough time to finish our work, etc. We live by clocks that tell us there's not enough time. Time is always lacking.

If you knew you were timeless, would you not approach your time in the moment a whole lot differently? If you knew that time was in the heavenly treasury and it never ended, would you not view your life completely differently? Would you not begin to enjoy your life everlasting more? See, that's why time is in the treasury. It has great value. However, isn't it true that Jesus defied time with the resurrection itself. Time said He was dead; but then He rose, so He beat the clock with time from the eternal treasury of Heaven.

There are many Scriptures about time from an earthly perspective. Time in the Greek is a special word, *chron*. When God talks about sowing into the spirit, receiving life everlasting, that's the Greek word *chron*, which means time is perpetual; it's from the beginning of time and runs its course. Other Greek words for time include *chronos*, which means space and time. There's also *kairos*, which means opportunity. There are several other "time" words. You're everlasting and you need to sow into your spirit in order to reap everlasting life.

Let's go to Galatians, because in these treasuries there are also *kairos* moments. *Chronos* is there, but at the same time so is *kairos*:

*Let us not become weary in doing good, for at the proper **time** we will reap a harvest if we do not give up. Therefore, as we have **opportunity**, let us do good to all people, especially to those who belong to the family of believers* (Galatians 6:9-10).

The word *kairos* is found in this particular Scripture, meaning that opportunities are part of the treasury. God gives certain seasons and certain times over the everlasting that produce certain amounts of fruit. As much as everlasting time is important, it is broken up into seasons of opportune times that when they come, we must take advantage of from an everlasting perspective. You don't take advantage of them because they're going to be gone, going to cease. You take advantage of them because they manifest in a season you live in the eternal realm. Does that make sense? It's time to change your thinking here.

ANOTHER KEY

Another key to accessing heavenly treasury—eternal rewards. Everlasting rewards in the earthly realm are extremely important. But there are also earthly rewards. There is a law of sowing and reaping that says if you work hard, you receive a blessing, right? That's a natural law, but it's also a spiritual law that manifests in the natural and brings forth fruit. But now listen to this; Matthew 6 describes the difference between earthly wages and eternal rewards.

This word "reward" is used two different times in these Scriptures given as both a positive and a negative. Let's take a look at what Matthew 6:1-4 says:

Be careful not to practice your righteousness in front of others *to be seen by them. If you do,* **you will**

have no reward from your Father in heaven. So when you give to the needy, do not announce it with trumpets, as the hypocrites do in the synagogues and on the streets, to be honored by others. Truly I tell you, they have received their reward in full. But when you give to the needy, do not let your left hand know what your right hand is doing, so that your giving may be in secret. Then **your Father, who sees what is done in secret, will reward you.**

Matthew 6 says the same thing about prayer and fasting. Why is this so important? Because if you're accessing the treasuries of Heaven, you have to understand—this is the key—that there's a correlation between being seen in the earthly realm and your reward in accordance with these Scripture verses in the Word of God.

The word "reward" is broken down into two Greek words. One is *misthos,* which means the pay a hired hand receives for service—an earthly reward. I do something and I get paid for it. Okay, that's how the earth operates.

But when you are not seen and you do something, then you can access the unseen rewards. That comes from the Greek word *shalam,* which means a recompense or a restoration, a yield. When you read in Matthew 6, you have to understand that those two Greek words for reward are used. One refers to performing well and receiving an earthly reward; but that's not accessing the treasuries of Heaven. The other refers to doing something good in secret and you receive an unseen reward. This is the reward that comes from the treasuries in Heaven.

Now that doesn't mean that it won't come into the natural and be a beautiful gift that you'll actually get your hands on, but it didn't come because you were paid for it. It came from Heaven; you touched it in the natural, but it is completely and entirely from the heavenly treasury. Now, you see, you can access the heavenly treasuries. You can receive by faith the keys to the heavenly treasury; you will be able to walk like Jesus did.

I need you to know that Jesus didn't care about time; after all, He was four days late to respond to Mary and Martha's plea for Him to come and see about their brother Lazarus. Yes, four days late. Yet He was still on time from a heavenly perspective. He accessed the heavenly treasury and brought forth a resurrection from the dead, this temporal existence. He saved the death of time. He brought back Lazarus' time on earth. He brought the everlasting from Heaven into the earthly realm. If He did it, you can too.

Now pray with me as we ask God to give, by faith, the supernatural sight to see the truth into the Word of God and know that you too have access to the heavenly treasuries: *Lord, please quicken the spirit and soul of this student of Your Word today and bring this reader the spiritual sight and revelatory wisdom to see into the heavenly treasuries and access them today.* Now, start practicing today. When you hear yourself pray, "Lord, I need some time. I'm feeling my body stress out right now; I'm sweating. Time is passing me by"—remember, that's a lack mentality. So, right away turn your mindset around and pray to access the treasuries of Heaven and bring everlasting time into the current temporal moment you are living in. "Lord, thank You for the time You've given me. Help me to use it for Your glory."

CHANGE YOUR MIND TO ACCESS HEAVEN

What has to change in order for us to access heavenly treasuries? The mind has to change. How does the mind change? Through the Word. You have to know the Word for your mind to change. You have to work the Word until it works for you. You have to work God's Word into your soul until all of a sudden, your spirit expands into soul prosperity and is so big that you say, "Give me my treasury now." You have to ask Him for it. Your heavenly Father, your Daddy sits on His throne waiting for the one who believes. The one who is going to come and say, "Dad, I know You have it. You have what I need." He's going to say, "I gave you My word. Will you now decree and declare that it is yours? If you do, it will come down for you."

We need to have confidence to come to the throne of grace knowing that the heavenly treasuries are open to us. In the next chapter you will learn how to release captives in your life through accessing the heavenly treasuries. We have much to learn about how to access heavenly blessings for ourselves and also for others. God wants you to not only access for yourself, but for others in need too.

CHAPTER 9

RELEASING CAPTIVES
THROUGH HEAVENLY
STRATEGIES

One of the ways we need to exercise our authority as citizens of Heaven is in the area of helping others to be released from captivity. Sometimes we are in a dark place in our minds and we need the Word of God to shed light. Sometimes our family or friends are in this place and we need the tools to help release them from captivity.

When I began to use these tools I am teaching you in this chapter, God began to release those around me. I would go into the rooms with the heavenly vats and pull out what each person needed to bless them. I would declare and decree and call these needed items into the earthly realm. This truly changed my thinking on how important it is to God for us to intercede for others and help them receive what they need from Heaven.

When you can help someone by accessing these heavenly vats on their behalf, you are truly fulfilling one of God's purposes on earth as an intercessor or one called to stand in the gap to release the captives. In this chapter, I show you how to release the heavenly vats of new grain, wine, oil, and gold into situations where people you love are being held captive.

INTERCEDE FOR THE CAPTIVES

We need to understand that darkness is not so much about what is around you. Many times, it's what's suffocating you on the inside. God wants to give you sight to see in the darkness. Darkness represents a level of captivity. We as the people of God are called not only to be free, but also to do what? To set other people free! God didn't just set you free for yourself. He set you free and He saved you that you might be the light that goes out and is in cooperation with Him, in cooperation with the Holy Spirit, to help bring salvation to another person.

Salvation comes when the blinders fall off people's eyes and they begin to see. When God calls us to be the change in our environments, we will notice warfare in our relationships. Difficult relationships reveal that you are not in sync with the other person. If you are not seeing eye to eye, there is a veil of darkness present. Now, of course, we all want to think that we're the ones who are seeing clearly and others are not. That may be truth. However, they may be seeing clearly and you may not be.

But when you come together as believers, God doesn't want you to get into a brawl because you disagree. That is not His will. He instead wants you to be the one who goes to the mountain and asks for supernatural sight to help release the captive person who is creating those issues in your life. Most of the time people do not want to pray for someone who is creating issues for them. But that's not how it works in the Kingdom of God, it's actually the opposite. *We must be willing to pray for those who persecute us and bless those who curse us* (see Matt. 5:44).

If you don't want to pray for someone, that is a clear sign to ask the Lord why. What happens next? God will reveal to you that there are places inside you that are hurt and troubled and you don't have the strength to pray for that person. But you can regain your strength through the joy of the Lord (see Neh. 8:10). God is going to supernaturally bring you into your place of joy and strength. No matter what kind of warfare you're going through, you will find time to rejoice in the Lord—and I say rejoice always!

Paul and Silas were chained inside a prison. But what did they do? They rejoiced! As they rejoiced, their chains began to break (Acts 16:25-26). We know that when we rejoice we are getting to the place where we are standing on the head of the devil and we are making a way. When we come to this place in our soul, we're not sitting there playing chess with the devil. No. We know that he's defeated and now we're going to step into the place of not only setting ourselves free, but setting others free too. We are releasing Heaven with our praise and rejoicing. And the best part? With that praising comes breaking the chains of bondage.

BREAK BONDAGES

One of the ways we can break the bondages over people's lives is to remember that we are heavenly beings first, and we are seated with God in heavenly places. This will keep our minds properly positioned from a heavenly perspective so that we can intercede on behalf of those who are in need and remember that their issues are earthly issues. We all must contend with the earth; however, God's desire is that even though our bodies are here on earth, our minds will be on Him and the heavenly realms.

If we are to help set other people free, we must take our proper positions just as Jesus did for us. We must assume our position and work from there. What was Jesus' position? In Hebrews 10:12-14, the Word says, *"But when this priest had offered for all time one sacrifice for sins, he sat down at the right hand of God, and since that time he waits for his enemies to be made his footstool. For by one sacrifice he has made perfect forever those who are being made holy."*

Jesus gave us access to the royal treasuries as our High Priest who shed His blood for us, and those who oppose Him and us are under our feet.

This is our position because He made the way, so we need to stand in this place when we are accessing the vats of Heaven. Do not get entangled in earthly affairs when you are going to the throne of grace to ask for the vats in Heaven to be opened to release a captive. You must stand knowing Jesus made the way and you do have access. When people start getting all earthly and temporal, let them be. You don't have to wrangle with that nonsense. You are better off keeping your position as God mandates and then calling Heaven down upon them.

Stop getting manipulated by worldly influence and start influencing the world. When you wrangle with the world, you become part of it and lose your authority in your mind. You cannot keep your confidence in calling down the heavenly vats if you don't maintain your positional authority. You must know your proper position and maintain it, not because of your good works but because of what Jesus did for you! He bought your position, so hold on to it. He needs you to be who He has called you to be, so others will be set free!

ACCESS THE HEAVENLY VATS

God's desire is to bring you into a place with people where you are going to help carry them from lack to prosperity. Yes, you are the citizen of Heaven who has been called to help bring from the heavenly vats, a supply that they need in the natural. God is saying, "I'm going to give you strength to go into My vats of Heaven and call down every resource needed—grain, wine, oil, gold, time—and bring it into the earthly realm on behalf of the person you're warring with." Wars start because of lack. A war only begins because people see lack, they don't see fullness. If you see fullness, then you have no reason to be complaining about anything. There's no reason for a war if you already have everything you need.

Wars start because you have something that I want or you've taken something from me and I need to have it. Instead of fighting, why not take authority and say, "I'm going to the place where all of our resources can be met and I'm going to pray it down for both of us." Now that takes some strength because you're probably feeling defeated and saying to yourself, *I'm so upset, I'm so weighted down, I can't get out of bed. Oh my gosh, somebody help me get out of this place.*

When warfare comes into a situation, and anytime there's fighting among the people of God, witchcraft is part of it; there are lying spirits pressing in on every part of your life. These demonic forces bind your faith and voice so you do not call out into being what is needed in that moment of distress. When that pressing begins, you don't want to do anything but stay in bed, or complain to your neighbor, or pick fights—because hurting people hurt people. If someone picks a fight with you, stop and say, "God, give me sight into this person. Something or someone has wounded this person and that's why

135

he/she is acting this way. God, I need to go to Heaven and get the resource that they need and pray it through until it's received."

God needs free people to help Him release the captives. It's most probable that some people around you are being held captive. You know how I know that? Because if your light is shining brightly, you're a magnet for the captives. Captives think you're awesome. They may not tell you that, but they do. They may be talking behind your back, they may be saying all kinds of things about you—for instance, that you're crazy—it is because they want what you have. But you have to be smart and see through their pettiness to see their need. Then you need to go to that place with God in prayer and prophesy and intercede and declare and decree what God shows you that they need.

Please don't go to them and whip out your Bible and throw Scripture verses in their face. I can tell you right now they will not listen to you because you are the voice that made them angry. Instead, take your supernatural warfare weapons and go into the zone where nobody can hear what you're saying except God. Say it to Him and He will move a mountain and make a change in the situation. After days or weeks or months of praying, there is deliverance! Anytime God sets captives free, someone remained persistent. Wars are not won in a second, they're won over time. But you'll get wiser and wiser as you remain faithful to take your stand.

As you keep praying for people, suddenly God will tell you the day when they are ready to hear what their need is and how God can meet it. They may even come to you and say, "You're not going to believe this, but my need has been met." You're going to say, "Yep. I believe it. You don't know this, but I've been secretly praying for you for the last month, that you would receive what your heart has been crying out. I'm glad you've finally got it." We need to decide that we're going to be warriors in that area. God wants to bring forth fruit in their lives, but He needs some midwives to help carry the load. Will you be that somebody who helps carry the load?

COACH OTHERS TO FREEDOM

When people are about ready to change and bring life from a dead place into the natural realm, they need a coach; they need someone to stand with them and say, "Breathe. You're going to make it. It's going to be all right." You have to have some encouragers in the room. You do not want anyone in the room with you while you're giving birth to say nasty or negative things to you. You want them out. That's when you say, "Doctor, call security and get this person out of here. I need encouragers around me." You need to have people surrounding you who are going to speak life to you and help carry the load. You need people to help you fight the good fight of faith. (See 1 Timothy 6:12; 2 Timothy 4:7.)

Prophetically this is what God is saying, "I want the people of God to come together and help carry the loads of one another and especially for the captives, so we can bring forth purpose and blessing from Heaven to earth. You can participate with Heaven to bring even your enemy's dreams forth; and as their dreams come forth, your dream is going to come forth as well." See, your dream comes at a cost and most of it is a cost of prayer. People may talk badly about you. Unfair things may happen to you. But the real cost to you is how much time are you going to remain in prayer in the heavenlies when everything in the earth is telling you to pay attention to it rather than pray. Every devil will say, "Look at me" and "Complain about me. But don't pray!"

God says, "Ezekiel, there are some things I want to show you." He was in a place where people were in captivity. They had been in captivity for a long time. The Bible says, *"In the twenty-fifth year of our captivity, at the beginning of the year, on the tenth day of the month, in the fourteenth year after the city was captured, on the very same day the hand of the Lord was upon me..."* (Ezek. 40:1 NKJV). This is what the prophet says:

> *In the visions of God He took me into the land of Israel and he set me on a very high mountain; on it toward the south was something like the structure of a city. He took me there, and behold, there was a man whose appearance was like the appearance of bronze. He had a line of flax and a measuring rod in his hand, and he stood in the gateway* (Ezekiel 40:2-3 NKJV).

This man said to Ezekiel, *"Son of man, look with your eyes and hear with your ears, and fix your mind on everything I show you; for you were brought here so that I might show them to you. Declare to the house of Israel everything you see"* (Ezek. 40:4 NKJV).

When we want to help release people from captivity and have Heaven invade their surroundings so they can be brought into the place where they can actually bring forth life from death, as in the purpose God has for them, we have to realize that God is going to show us when we ask Him. We need to ask God, "What is it that they need to get and where is it that You're calling them to be, God?" In other words, when you see their maladaptive behavior, you see their addiction, you see their fear, you see their worry, you see their frustration, you see the pain they're going through, and it is too much to handle. We must cry out, "Abba Father, free them, and tell me what these captive people need!"

DECLARE AND DECREE
PROVISION FOR THE NEED

The Word says that God's going to show you what they need. He's going to give you sight in the darkness. You will be able to see what is needed. Why? Because our heavenly Father wants to set people free. He sent His Son, Jesus Christ, so that we can be positioned to be the ones who set others free. God's not withholding this information from you. If you come to the throne and you ask Him to tell you what a person needs, God will show you. We say to God, "Show me so I can ask You for them because they can't ask for themselves; they're too hardheaded, stubborn, and prideful and they don't want to hear what it is that I have to say." God will show you, as He showed Ezekiel. Then you're going to stand on the Word. Make no mistake, He will give you eyes to see and ears to hear what's necessary.

Then the Word says, *"...Declare to the house of Israel everything you see"* (Ezek. 40:4). Now here's the key—when God shows you what someone needs, you have to declare and decree it to the spirit realm. This is wisdom; watch your ability to declare and decree it to them, for it's all about timing. Sometimes people take offense at what you're saying and don't believe you. Because they're angry at you, you become the object of their wrath. But you are declaring and decreeing it to the heavens. You sow God's Word to the heavens. Hosea 2:21-23 says:

> *"It shall come to pass in that day that I will answer," says the Lord; "I will answer the heavens, and they shall answer the earth. The earth shall answer with grain, with new wine, and with oil; they shall answer Jezreel. Then I will sow her for Myself in the earth, and I will have mercy on her who had not obtained mercy; then I will*

*say to those who were not My people, 'You are My people!'
And they shall say, 'You are my God!'"* (Hosea 2:21-23
NKJV).

In due time, God will give you the ability to declare to them the
hours prayed for them, or you might not even be the voice, He may
choose someone else to do it. Just remember that you may be the one
who spends hours praying for someone, but somebody else may be
the one who gets to tell them or gets to see the results from Heaven.
You have to be willing not to be prideful enough to say it has to be
me. It doesn't have to be you, but you are willing. You just do what
you're supposed to do. You talk to Heaven and then let Heaven talk
to whoever Heaven needs to talk to. When we sow to the Spirit, we
will reap everlasting life (see Gal. 6:8 NKJV).

Now, let me take you to another set of Scriptures that shows you
how this system works. We have Ezekiel, and he saw, and he heard,
and then he began to declare. I also mentioned the Book of Hosea.
Let me give you some more in-depth information about the importance of the Book of Hosea for releasing Heaven into your situation.

The Book of Hosea revolves around the fact that Hosea, the
prophet, was asked by God to marry Gomer. Gomer was a prostitute. God set up the whole scenario to bring into the earthly realm a
heavenly level of visibility for all to see, so people could witness the
compassion of God and how God operates when He works through
exemplifying His love for His adulterous people.

Hosea's love for Gomer and his desire to take in this prostitute,
while allowing her to be unfaithful to him, is an example of God's
love for us when we run away from Him and are adulterous. God is
ever constant in His love for us; He stays with us.

The beginning of Hosea chapter 2 reveals that God was angry with the unfaithfulness of Israel. Hosea mentions the vats in Heaven; he talks about new grain, new wine, and new oil. He says that they're there, but that He is going to put a hold on them. In other words, Israel, you have no access to them. It was part of a discipline. But near the end of the Book of Hosea, after there is repentance on the part of Israel, there is now full redemption and access to the vats of Heaven. This is what God says:

> *In that day I will make a covenant for them with the beasts of the field, with the birds of the air, and with the creeping things of the ground. Bow and sword of battle I will shatter from the earth, to make them lie down safely* (Hosea 2:18 NKJV).

In other words, God's bringing the blessings back.

He says, *"I will betroth you to Me forever; yes, I will betroth you to Me in righteousness and justice, in lovingkindness and mercy; I will betroth you to Me in faithfulness, and you shall know the Lord"* (Hos. 2:19-20 NKJV). God's coming back here and He's saying, "Israel, listen, I love you; and because I love you, you get all of this too." Although He was angry and upset and had to instill a discipline, in the end He returns to them after Israel's repentance and in the act of redemption.

THE HEAVENLY VATS OPEN

Then He says, *"'It shall come to pass in that day, that I will answer,' says the Lord; 'I will answer the heavens, and they shall answer the earth. The earth shall answer with grain, with new wine, and with oil; they shall answer Jezreel'"* (Hos. 2:21-22 NKJV). The name Jezreel means "God sows," it means God Himself sows.

God says in the next verse, *"And I will sow her unto me in the earth; and I will have mercy upon her that had not obtained mercy; and I will say to them which were not my people, Thou art my people; and they shall say, Thou art my God"* (Hos. 2:23 KJV).

When you pray for those who are captive, you are sowing the Word and you're sowing with a determination and a full-heart feeling of wanting to see the fulfillment and the bringing forth of purpose and destiny for you and this other person. You're sowing it to the heavens, and the heavens hear it, because the heavens hear the earth and the people in the earth praying.

Then the Word says, God sows to the earth and the heavenly vats of new grain, wine, and oil are dispersed. The vats hold the resources needed to bring it forth. But how does that happen? One has to sow. You have to be one who sows to Heaven with the Word by declaring, decreeing, praying, and standing firm. The devil's going to come at you hard when he sees you doing this. He may send a few demons to kick you around and tell you you're no good. He wants to shut down your prayer life. That's when you need to say, "No, devil, I'm going to pray even more." When you pray, then God says, "I'm going to release these things and then I, God, Jezreel, am going to sow into the earth. I, God, am going to sow into the issue that is taking place here. I, God, am going to release what is needed. It is going to come in time and you're going to believe it by faith and then it all is going to start to come forth."

You have to be determined as one who has been called to set the captives free—that you indeed are going to bring a praise to the Lord, a word to the Lord, a declaration and a decree to God. When you make that determination, you cannot be stopped!

The Word says that the Lord spoke to Jeremiah saying:

> *"Again, there shall be heard in this place—of which you say, 'It is desolate, without man and without beast'— in the cities of Judah, in the streets of Jerusalem that are desolate, without man and without inhabitant and without beast, the voice of joy and the voice of gladness, the voice of the bridegroom and the voice of the bride, the voice of those who will say: 'Praise the Lord of hosts, for the Lord is good, for His mercy endures forever'—and of those who will bring the sacrifice of praise into the house of the Lord. For I will cause the captives of the land to return as at the first," says the Lord* (Jeremiah 33:10-11 NKJV).

That is a place of captivity.

God has made us promises. Just as Israel was captive at one point, He brought them back to Himself in His love—just as you were captive at one point, when you knew nothing about the love of God. This is because you can be saved in your spirit, but your soul can still be in a place of suffering from great trauma. The part of the soul that is dark needs His light to shine on it so what is hurting can be seen and dealt with.

The Word says that all shall want to prophesy (see Joel 2:28). What that means is that inside you is the Holy Spirit Himself and He wants to come forth and He wants to speak a word; He wants to show you something. We need God to give us sight to help those who are in need. We need the Holy Spirit to show us their darkness, the trauma of their soul, and what need they have so that as citizens of Heaven we may help those in need to cross over the threshold and bring forth purpose, destiny, and peace into their lives.

If you become a midwife for someone, your dream is going to come to pass. If someone becomes a midwife for you, then their dream will come to pass. But someone has to stand up and say, "I'm going to release the captives and I'm going to do it in prayer, in seeking God and in breaking the strongholds by going to the throne of God and asking for a release of new grain, new wine, new oil, gold, and time."

I don't know about you, but I am not going to be messing with flesh and blood. I will go to the only place that can make a difference. Salvation comes to people because others have been praying for them for a very long time. Somebody sowed into Heaven, and Heaven heard; then Heaven turned around and sowed back because it was the will of Heaven to do so.

Do you want to see peace in your home? Do you want to see peace at your job? Do you want to see peace and growth and the bringing forth of the blessing of God, then *never stop praying* because that is the only way that anything is ever going to change on this earth. That's the only way! You're the change agent. God is putting in your hands tenacity to pray, no matter the circumstances. Spend some time rejoicing, having the joy of the Lord within you as you go about your everyday life. No matter what you're faced with, put a smile on your face and say, "Yea, hallelujah!" Because you know where you're going tonight, to the throne to pray it down.

You are a citizen of Heaven and God is going to use you to help others bring forth their dreams. We need people willing to carry these dreams across the threshold. Fight the good fight with prayer, declaring, decreeing, believing, and especially with the sacrifice of praise. This principle of sowing and reaping is a universal principle. We must sow to the heavens and then they sow to the earth. If you want earth to change, you must sow to Heaven. This is a main principle in accessing the heavenly realms and releasing the supernatural treasuries of Heaven.

CHAPTER 10

YOU ARE ENOUGH

If you want heavenly encounters to be released into your environ-ment so the supernatural can come, you must realize that you are "enough" and God can use you. God loves you no matter what; and when you come to realize this fact, you will walk in open-heaven encounters and really step into changing your environment.

Whenever God asks me to participate with Him in changing an environment, I have to come to a place of focusing on the substance inside me—praising Him from my innermost being. In order to do that I must like myself. I went through a stage in my life when I had self-hatred and it was hard for me to love myself. God had me spend hours in His presence in order to heal that brokenness in my life.

During those years of resting in silence with Him, I learned to focus on Him no matter the situation I was faced with. If my envi-ronments were unhealthy or negative, I would simply focus on Him and joy would rise up, and I would begin to praise Him. Then I could no longer see my tough environment.

Because God wants us to be glory portals to bring Heaven to earth, we must not allow our situations or environments to control us, we must focus on Him and let Him change our environments. We must not become intimidated by the negativity or harshness of our environment because God has us in these environments to be used of Him to bring heavenly encounters so He can change the environment.

The Lord taught me to focus on Him and not look at my surroundings when He wants the glory to fall in a place and have a heavenly encounter come to change the environment. He wants you to learn to focus on Him. If your home life is crazy, you are to keep your eyes on Him and let Him change the environment. You agree with Him about what He wants to do, then you don't look at the change, you just look at Him, and He makes the change. When my kids were all under 5 years old and in diapers, we were living in Whidbey Island, Washington, and my husband was frequently away on deployments. Sometimes I would sit in a corner and pray in tongues as they just crawled all over me.

My circumstances were tough being a young mom and alone and 3,000 miles away from family who could help me with our children. But I learned to rest in God and He would give me the strength to change my environment by praying in tongues until His Spirit fell in my home and the kids became quiet and at peace—or until I got the strength in an overflow in my soul to keep going. God taught me the basics of heavenly encounters because I needed those heavenly encounters in my difficult times.

The focus on God kept me at peace while He made the change to bring peace in our home. I learned to pray heaven down when the children were young. I learned to pray for my husband and watch

God change him. I could not do it, only God could. One of the disciplines I practiced frequently was the discipline of solitude. I will share more about this discipline in my next book, *21 Days to the Supernatural Life.*

You see, God wants you to trust Him, trust that He will change your situation. But you need to position yourself in prayer and focus on Him with all of your substance so that God can move. Then when God speaks, you do as He says and agree with Him in faith—and boom, your environment changes.

Everyone wants to change, to improve their environment, but the key is to first change your focus. A steady focus on God will change your environment, not focusing on your environment. We have it backward. God trained me to make Heaven first and then my earthly surroundings will change, not the other way around. This is some wisdom for watching Heaven come to earth and the supernatural to begin. If you want the supernatural, you must sow into the Spirit first, then you can reap from the Spirit. The apostle Paul says, *"Whoever sows to please their flesh, from the flesh will reap destruction; whoever sows to please the Spirit, from the Spirit will reap eternal life"* (Gal. 6:8).

LIVING IN THE OVERFLOW

In this chapter I explain how you are complete and whole in Christ. That you are "enough" in Him and *He loves the substance inside you.* That substance is you. When you know the substance grown inside you, you will have the confidence to pray for Heaven to come into your environments.

So, what is substance? Substance is the depth of your soul and body, and the handing over of it to God. You may be asking yourself,

How does this work? Well, in your spirit, you are brand-new if you've received Jesus as your Lord and Savior, but your soul is in a process of transformation. In Proverbs, the Word says:

> *Honor the Lord with your wealth* [substance], *with the firstfruits of all of your crops* [increase]*; then your barns will be filled to overflowing, and your vats will brim over with new wine* [with new opportunities] (Proverbs 3:9-10).

Do you want to live in the overflow anointing? Do you want to see the supernatural invade the natural? If yes, then the revelation in this proverb is a vital key. *You must learn how to honor the Lord with your substance.* When you do, your barn, or your soul, is going to be filled to overflowing, and new opportunities are going to come to you. But, when does this happen?

When God says "honor Me" with your substance, He means honor Him with your spirit, your soul, and your body. He wants all of you. He wants your time, your talent, your testimony, and your treasure. He wants the entire you to come to Him for honor. He finds you honorable and worthy to give Him yourself. He says you are enough. We give Him our spirit at the moment we receive Jesus and our old self dies on the Cross with Christ and is buried and resurrected in Christ (see Rom. 6:3). We are made new in our spirit as new creatures in Christ, but the soul with all of its sin and iniquity is in need of change (see 2 Cor. 5:17).

Our soul is messed up from the Fall of humankind. It's broken, hurting, and gets offended. It goes through anger and spurts of frustration. It has a lot to deal with because it's in a broken place—and all human beings are in this state. No one is free from a broken soul.

But when God says, "Honor Me with your substance," He is saying, "I want your substance, I want your wealth, as in your power, your ability, everything about you." This is actually rooted in the fact that He wants us to obtain our heavenly treasure, or substance, through an understanding of our and even our idols, and putting Him first by repenting and turning from them. Our substance involves our repentance, changing our mind, and our willingness to have our soul transformed into the likeness of His Son, Jesus.

SUBSTANCE COMES WHEN WE TURN AWAY FROM IDOLS

We are going to do a word search deep into the Hebrew language, so you can really see what the word "substance" means. When you can grasp this truth, you will be positioning yourself for a release of substance inside you that will change your atmospheres.

God is saying that you are enough, *even with* the iniquity and the sin that you have in your soul. Now, that may be difficult to believe. This does not make sense to judgmental people; but it makes sense to people who know how much they have been forgiven and understand the grace of God—and that grace is through faith, not of works (see Eph.2:8-9).

When we look into the word "substance," we must come from an understanding that God knows humanity's roots of idol worship. Idols are not little gold calves we put on our altar and bow down to. They are things in our soul that we worship like our needs for provision, protection, and acceptance. Throughout our lifetime, we develop patterns in our lives to get our needs met.[1]

For example, let's say you need acceptance very badly in order to feel good about yourself; you will develop a pattern in your life to get that acceptance. Maybe you feel compelled to buy coffee for everyone at your office so they will accept you. And you think that the day you decide not to buy coffee, you will not be loved by them. So, you put yourself in bondage to the habit of buying coffee, even to the point that when your spouse says stop buying the coffee for everyone at the office, you can't because it has become your fix for attention and acceptance by your peers. It is meeting a deep need for love, so you put yourself in a place of bondage to it. Now the good thing has become an idol because you can't stop it and others are being hurt by your habit. In and of itself, buying coffee for everyone is generally a nice gesture, but for you it is a law and you must do it or else you will not like yourself. That is an example of an idol even though it may have an appearance of being a good thing.

We make idols out of bad things too like drugs, pornography, gambling; overindulgence in anything can become an idol. When we choose to stand up and turn from these idols or we smash them or say, "No more idols in my life," that develops a strength that causes us to be able to honor God and bring God what He wants, which is a total heart and soul of repentance that forms into a substance in our souls that honors God.

You'll never really know the strength inside you until you say no to an idol in your life. It's in the test; it's in the wrestling that you win and understand what you're made of. You may fall, I don't know how many times, when it comes to that idol; but when you take the time to allow God to strengthen you with His power, and you actually turn from that thing, you are being instilled with the *substance* that is honoring to Him. You are enough in Him and God wants all of you!

HEBRAIC ROOTS OF "SUBSTANCE"

Before we start defining "substance," I want you to look in a mirror at yourself and see this person who is in existence right now. You may see someone who is accomplished or is okay with God and moving toward purpose and destiny. You may look in the mirror and not see this person at all. But no matter who you see, you had a beginning or a start and it was before you knew Jesus as your Lord and Savior. Now that you do know Him, you have a starting point. If you have not received Jesus as Messiah, as your Deliverer, then you need to ask Him now to come into your heart as Romans says:

> If you declare with your mouth, "Jesus is Lord," and believe in your heart that God raised him from the dead, you will be saved. For it is with your heart that you believe and are justified, and it is with your mouth that you profess your faith and are saved (Romans 10:9-10).

So, salvation of the spirit is the starting point for this teaching. You probably agree that we each have a starting point with God, a place and time where we became brand-new in our spirit. Now He is working on our soul—which is comprised of our mind, will, and emotions. The soul is what we need to change for His glory and is part of our substance.

Let's go to the Hebrew root of the word "substance" found in the Scriptures in Proverbs 3:9-10. There are three Hebrew words that make up "substance" in that passage of Scripture: *hon, on,* and *aven.* The word "substance" first comes from the Hebrew root word, *hon,* which is defined as wealth or enough, which comes from a root word *on,* which is defined as ability, force, or power. This word goes deeper into the Hebrew root word *aven,* which means to pant, as in vain, and strictly nothingness, trouble, vanity, wickedness, idol, affliction, unrighteous, unjust, iniquity, sorrow.

Now I want you to picture a tree. The deepest root of the Hebrew word, which is the root of the tree, is *aven,* and it stays below the ground; then there are additional words built on top of it such as *on* and *hon.* Now stay with me as I explain why this is relevant to you.

The word "substance," which means enough, at its very root also means *aven* or to pant in vain, like you're working so hard with a false idol, like wrestling because you are a failure; or strictly nothingness, trouble, vanity, wickedness, idols, affliction, unrighteousness, injustice, iniquity, sorrow. What this means is that our starting point from birth is one of working hard, loving idols, and feeling like a failure. That's our root system. Sounds like we need a Savior, right? We know we need a Savior simply because we are the generations that have come from the Fall of humankind—the Fall of Adam and Eve. Now God is moving us from *aven* to a place of *hon,* meaning wealth and enough.

When we become *hon,* we are at a place where we have learned to rest in the Spirit of the Lord and we are giving our all to Him, as in a presentation of spirit, soul, and body. We are in a process of transformation, but we are resting as He does the work in and through us to make us into a substance that is for His glory. This glory holds our time, talent, treasure, and testimony, and we are not holding back anything. We are one with God, even with our iniquity and sin as a root, because it has been overcome by the blood of Jesus. Now we rest in His grace because He, for us, has conquered sin, death, and the grave in our souls. We are more than conquerors through Christ Jesus (see Rom. 8:37). That's exactly what God says. All of this "conquering power" is comprised into the word "substance"—it is now part of your identity in Christ. So what we learn is that we rise from the Hebrew root *aven* to be overcomers, and that is our "enough" or substance that we offer to God.

YOUR SOUL IS TRANSFORMING

There's a correlation between substance and the level of humility where you are pained by what is going on around you and where you turn from your idols and walk away from the things that are crying out for your attention. You walk away from those things in a way that is different now, as a result of what you have faced and now overcome.

So basically, because we begin life with *aven* in all of us, we start out with strictly nothingness, trouble, vanity, wickedness, idols, affliction, unrighteousness, injustice, iniquity, sorrow, all of these kinds of things. And that is what Jesus Himself, the great Redeemer, is going to free us from and build in us which is the glory substance that He wants.

I don't know about you, but I would've just pulled out the root in our souls and started with a whole new tree. Why mess with that thing? Why mess with something that was in iniquity and trouble and wickedness and all of that? Well, God is the lover of our soul, and because we start with a depraved soul, He came to transform our soul through a process from *aven*, to *on*, and to *hon*. He cares for us by making a new creation in our spirit and that is what He does to begin the process of now healing the soul with its wounds from *aven*. Let's look at Romans 6:3-5 (NKJV):

> *Or do you not know that as many of us as were baptized into Christ Jesus were baptized into His death? Therefore we were buried with Him through baptism into death, that just as Christ was raised from the dead by the glory*

of the Father, even so we also should walk in newness of life. For if we have been united together in the likeness of His death, certainly we also shall be in the likeness of His resurrection (NKJV).

He makes us new in the deepest recesses of our being, our spirit. This is what the apostle Paul is referring to that was buried in Romans 6—your unregenerate spirit self; and now you are born again, a regenerate spirit that became new, and is now alive in Christ.

But your soul did not become new when you became born again, it is still a work in progress and in transformation; therefore, you need to understand God wants your whole substance, which includes your new born-again spirit, and your transforming soul that He is changing from *aven*, to *on*, and to *hon*, and then finally to your flesh, or body. You can read more about soul transformation in my book, *Soul Transformation: Your Personal Journey*, which walks you through the processes of soul transformation.

This root system of *aven* in our soul is actually needed for God to bring you the strength that He wants and for the substance He desires. It's a needed part of His whole plan. The Fall of humankind was part of His greater plan. It wasn't His will, but He incorporated it into His plan and Jesus agreed to die to liberate us from this very root. He took our choices and He wrapped them into His sovereign will. It wasn't His perfect will, but He wrapped it into His sovereignty so that He could build us from the ground up. The following are a few Scriptures that make up the Hebrew word *aven*, so you can see how *aven* is in all of us.

Wash your heart from evil, O Jerusalem, that you may be saved. How long will your wicked thoughts lodge within you? For a voice declares from Dan, and proclaims wick-edness [aven] *from Mount Ephraim* (Jeremiah 4:14-15 NASB).

Woe to those who scheme iniquity [aven], *who work out evil on their beds! When morning comes, they do it, for it is in the power of their hands* (Micah 2:1 NASB).

But do not resort to Bethel and do not come to Gilgal, nor cross over to Beersheba; for Gilgal will certainly go into captivity and Bethel will come to trouble [aven] (Amos 5:5 NASB).

Is there iniquity [aven] *in Gilead? Surely they are worth-less. In Gilgal, they sacrifice bulls, yes, their altars are like the stone heaps beside the furrows of the field* (Hosea 12:11 NASB).

In Hosea 12:11, the word "iniquity" is *aven*. He's using these Scriptures to say these people are iniquitous. These people are sinners. These people are worshipping false idols. That's the root here. Then we move on to the branches.

The next word that involves substance is the Hebrew word *on*, and it means to be focused on your efforts. So now we're at wick-edness and we're trying to work it out with our effort. That's *on*, which means vigor, power, physical strength of men, and behemoth. Behemoth is a strong force. So this is a power that comes from effort as you're working off the iniquity. In Genesis the Word says, *"Reuben, you are my firstborn; my might and the beginning of my strength..."* (Gen. 49:3 NASB). So God is saying, *"Listen, you started with aven, and you worked it out with your own effort. You're developing* some strength." Now you're walking in the Hebrew word *on,* which is strength.

This word for strength is also used in Deuteronomy 21:17 (NASB), *"But he shall acknowledge the firstborn, the son of the unloved, by giving him a double portion of all that he has, for he is the beginning of his strength [on]; to him belongs the right of the firstborn."* Notice how these Scriptures are talking about strength relative to the firstborn. Why? Because the root system is where everything starts, and then what comes up is the first growth. Strength is developed from the pain of iniquity. Nothing changes in your life if there's no pain.

We get to a place where we start trying to work it out; we are taking the initiative, even if it is fleshly, and that is a strength that God Himself desires in us. This is actively processing through our transformation. The good news is, although it is a work of the flesh at this stage, He's still causing it for our good. This is what it says in this Scripture, *"And smote all the firstborn in Egypt, the first issue of their virility [on]..."* (Ps. 78:51 NASB). This means their strength, in the tents of Ham. That's the Hebrew word *on.*

And in this Scripture, *"He also struck down all the firstborn in their land, the first fruits of all their vigor [on]"* (Ps. 105:36 NASB). Although we are bringing forth a fleshly strength that is working and is toiling and is trying to figure out these false idols and all of that, God is going to use it. It's part of your substance. All of this is part of who you are. It is the substance that God Himself wants for His glory. The Hebrew word *on* can also be referenced to a type of strength of God as we see in the scriptures below. It is a strength that produces overflow.

> *Lift up your eyes on high and see who has created these stars, the One who leads forth their host by number, He*

calls them all by name; because of the greatness of His might and the strength [on] *of His power, not one of them is missing* (Isaiah 40:26 NASB).

He gives strength [on] *to the weary, and to him who lacks might He increases power* (Isaiah 40:29 NASB).

STRENGTH TO PERSEVERE

God can mix our natural strength with His supernatural and give us an *on* strength above the *aven,* or iniquity of our souls. He takes your love for idols, your iniquity, all of that, and as you're working it out, He creates a strength within that He calls a substance.

These last Scriptures, which encompass substance and are at the top of the heap, use the Hebrew word *hon.* This is where we see the strength beginning to come forward, where we are pressing into victory. This Hebrew word, *hon,* is the word for substance; we see it used in Deuteronomy 1:41, and here it means to be ready.

> *Then you said to me, "We have sinned against the Lord; we will indeed go up and fight, just as the Lord our God commanded us." And every man of you girded on his weapons of war, and regarded* [hon] *it as easy to go up into the hill country* (Deuteronomy 1:41 NASB).

That word "regarded" is the word *hon* here; and to paraphrase, it means to be ready to have gone from a place of pain to a place of pressing. It means you've walked into this place where your substance is, where all your own weapons are, and all the effort that you poured into it. All of these things that you've been striving and pressing and wrestling with have now become a valuable substance; you are now regarded as a soul that is transforming and positioning itself to honor God.

This is a journey, as nothing about the root or the branches is immediate. It takes time, and it takes repentance. It starts with recognizing that you need a Savior. Trying to work it all out on your own doesn't work. God comes into your world and says, "It's not all about trying to work it out on your own, but what I will do is use your efforts of working toward holiness, son and daughter, until you can get yourself to a place where now we can press in and win that victory together." That's substance.

Once you have come through this pain to pressing, God will say to you, "Now you have a substance that I want, that I want to reconcile to Myself. What's going to honor Me is when you bring it all to Me." What did we learn in that process? We learn how to turn away from our idols.

When you bring God substance, that's the fullness of what you've learned in your soul. False idols are going to take you down, but if you fight against them, God is going to take all of that substance, which then becomes your wealth, your ability, your power, and your strength. All of that becomes what He says, "Honor Me with this, and give it to Me." It is the worst of you worked out and becoming now the best of you. Apostle Paul tells us, *"continue to work out your salvation with fear and trembling"* (Phil. 2:12).

So what's the long and short of this? Don't throw away the pain and suffering in your soul; it is producing character. Read and absorb the wisdom in Second Peter 1:5-9 (NKJV):

> *But also for this very reason, giving all diligence, add to your faith virtue, to virtue, to virtue knowledge, to knowledge self-control, to self-control perseverance, to perseverance godliness, to godliness brotherly kindness, and to brotherly kindness love. For if these things are yours and abound, you will be neither barren nor unfruitful in the*

*knowledge of our Lord Jesus Christ. For he who lacks these
things is shortsighted, even to blindness, and has forgotten
that he was cleansed from his old sins.*

Love every bit of who you were and who you are now because
all of it brings God glory. He is bigger than your mess. Everything
that you've been through in your life has brought you to the place
of substance. He wants the substance! That's what He wants.
He wants your substance. He wants *all* of you. You are enough.
There's enough inside you to glorify Him. It's not about perfection. It's about what He works in and through you with His grace
to accept iniquity and to raise it up. I only know that God would do
that through His Son. There's nobody else on this planet or in any
other sphere that could possibly take all those rags and make them
into riches.

Then He will call you unto Himself, "Honor Me with the substance of who you are." I mean, really, how does that make you feel?
He loves you for who you really are. There is substance to you. It
came because you had to work it out. It didn't come to you because
it was easy. It came to you because you cried. It came to you because
you said you had to leave that idol, and you didn't want to leave it. It
came to you when life was difficult. It came to you when you felt like
you had nothing but lack and a whole lot of field that you still had to
work. That's the substance that God has brought forth from inside
you. That's what He wants you to honor Him with.

There was a time when I understood substance differently. I
understood substance as my coming to the table with some kind of
perfection, some kind of clean slate. That was incorrect thinking.
Now I understand substance is what we have to work out with God,
and He's okay with that. I learned from this word study that God

loves me with all my mess; He's okay with it, because that's the fullness of the substance that He wants.

How does that make you feel when you know you don't have to be perfect to come to God? That He says to you, "I'll take you as you are." Just like that. He says, "I'm going to turn you into someone who has value to Me." I'll paraphrase what God says in Proverbs 3:9-10, "Honor Me with yourself." Along with that, you're honoring Him with even your past iniquity and false idols; when you choose to say no to those desires, God says, "Now you've honored Me. The strength from *aven* to *on* to *hon* has you now in the place where you can honor Me and Me alone."

What did you learn? You learned what an idol is. You learned what sucked the life out of your time, your talent, your treasure, your testimony. You looked at what was tearing you down, that was messing up your life, and you said, "I'm turning away from that."

God says, "Now, that's what I want!" But isn't it amazing that He doesn't throw it out? He wants the whole mold. It's a root part of who you are. Your confessions and your repentance came from a place where you learned a lesson. You realized that what you had your hands in was no good. That's part of your story. That's part of your substance. That's why substance is time, talent, treasure, and testimony. It's the fullness of who you are. God says, "I want all of you. You are enough for Me, just as you are."

YOU ARE INDEED ENOUGH

Now I want you to say, "I am enough just as I am. God wants me and loves me just as I am." Amen. Hallelujah! This teaching on substance is vital to learn, because as a child of God, what hurts God the most is when we honor graven images, when we put them on our little altars and we bow down to them. This hurts Him. But when we turn from them and turn toward Him, then He feels the honor. It's that way in our earthly relationships as well. For example, in marriage relationships, when we turn from a negative idol, we honor the other person. That's real. That's real honor and respect for our spouse. I'm going to say no to that. I'm going to say yes to this.

I want you to leave this teaching knowing one thing—God chose, in your soul, not to throw it all out. He started new with your spirit, but He left you in your earthsuit that needs to grow in strength, in power, in wisdom, in might, in holiness, and in glory. He left you in a place where He could still hang out with you while He grew you up.

He could have cleaned us all up in an instant. He didn't do it. He basically says to us, "I want to be your friend right where you are, but I'm going to make you right in the process." Think about the fact that it is God's grace on your life that is developing a substance inside you that will bring Him honor. Learn to say no to the idols, or the totality of your substance will not be brought forth in the way God wants it to be brought forth. There's a lesson to be learned here. As you're growing from *aven* to *on* to *hon*, things should be getting easier, and your burdens lighter, because you're now learning to say no to ungodly idols that kill and say you're not enough.

The Word says, *"Honor the Lord with your possessions* [substance], *and the firstfruits of all of your increase; so your barns will be filled with plenty, and your vats will overflow with new wine* [with new opportunities]" (Prov. 3:9-10 NKJV). So now that you learned to be part of His process of honoring Him through giving your substance to Him, which is all of you, the good, bad, and the ugly, then He says to give Him "...*the firstfruits of all your increase*" (Prov. 3:9 NKJV).

From our substance comes a release of increase, and He wants the first of it, which is honorable to Him. God always calls for first things in His Word. When we practice firstfruits and give our best to God first, we are stepping into a principle that releases Heaven to earth and shifts our atmosphere. Every time we begin a new month, or a new year, or a new job, or a new business, you are to give God the whole of something or a firstfruit.

This is called the principle of firstfruits. God is telling us if we want to see *our vats bursting with new wine and new opportunities,* then we need to give our substance, our firstfruits, and then our barn, our soul, and our homes or what we manage will burst open with more wine—more new opportunities for growth and advancement (see Prov. 3:10 NKJV). God is not stagnant. Heaven is always moving! If we want to infect our natural environments with releasing Heaven, we must make sure we follow the principle of substance, and firstfruits.

When we offer our firstfruits to the Lord, we are to *zakar* the Lord, which means we are to remember Him. In Deuteronomy the Word says, *"But remember the Lord your God, for it is He who gives you the ability to produce wealth, and so confirms His covenant, which He swore to your ancestors, as it is today"* (Deut. 8:18). This word "remember" is the Hebrew word *zakar,* which means to mark as in a male or first. We are to remember God each time He gives us increase from Heaven so we will not fall into the trap of taking too much for ourselves and thinking our own hands produced this wealth.

God has made your substance and given you the new wine opportunities that are before you. Your soul has become prosperous and now prosperity will begin to fall from Heaven. New wine opportunities have fallen from the heavenly vats, and now is the time to give

Him honor and thanksgiving by giving back to Him what He gave you. If you want to see Heaven come to earth and heavenly encounters begin where you are, you need to sow into Heaven with faith and giving. What happens then? Heaven will open up to you and will begin to return heavenly riches along with more grain, wine, and oil from Heaven.

God wants to create supernatural environments, but you must know who you are in His eyes. You must know your true identity and know that you are enough for Him to use for His glory—then heavenly encounters will be revealed in your life.

CHAPTER 11

ANGEL TURNAROUND

Do you remember in Chapter 2 how I shared with you about our church building and how much warfare we had to go through to actually possess the land? Well, angels were a key piece in the possession of the property. When we saw how difficult it was to possess the land, we called on the angel armies to come and assist us in taking that property. Every time we had an empty seat in our sanctuary, we asked the angels to fill it so that we could move ahead into the new building. We went to the new building and worked on it daily.

We prayed all over it every day, and many times we would congregate in the far back room of the building and it was filled with angels. There was so much peace in that one room. I could see the many angels there; they would stand guard day and night while we worked on the building—even before we actually received the certificate of occupancy and moved in. Every time people walked into the back room, they would say, "Wow, this is amazing. I feel the presence of God!" Yes, those angels harbored God's presence and kept watch day and night so that no enemy forces would gain more ground and push back our efforts.

Whenever the project would stagnate, we would pray again that God would send the warring angels to come in and move the property forward. Then we would feel the stagnation in the spirit realm stop and the work would begin to flow again. When you are dealing with contractors, city and county building plans and ordinances, and all the government bureaucracy involved, there are many times when a project will slow down. We just kept pressing night and day and calling on the Holy Spirit and angels of the Lord to sustain us and move the project forward.

The enemy did not want that property in our hands because that would mean no one could attend the bar anymore. Now it was God's house! We called it the house of restoration and transformation because what was dead was now alive. All we did was to the glory of God—and God used us and the angels to possess the property.

Even today there is a portal to the far right of our altar and I can still see it open and the angels ascending and descending in our sanctuary. Sometimes they come out and go into our foyer area and even outside on the street. We ask them to come into our services each week and fan the flame of fire, peace, and holiness, and they help change the atmosphere. We have many angel sightings at Freedom Destiny Church. We love to have them with us as they carry the glory of the Lord and open the heavens for us at each service.

Sometimes when the sound is off or the frequencies are rough in the building, we ask them to sing with us and we can hear the angelic hosts singing and joining with us in song. It is harmonious and beautiful. We know when they are there. Sometimes they come in and sit in the empty seats as we invite them, and they stand guard and worship with us or bring healing or holy fire for baptism. The angelic hosts are a daily part of our congregation.

ANGELS ON ASSIGNMENT

Now in this chapter, I share with you the power of the angels to bring Heaven to earth for the glory of God. We are all assigned an angel or angels to help us carry out the plans and purposes of Heaven on earth, our Kingdom assignments. These assignments sometimes need help from God's angels. My husband and I and Freedom Destiny Church were given an assignment in 2016 to occupy territory for the Lord that was considered dead. Through the power of God inside our Church and through angel armies, we were positioned to ambush the enemy and his plans! We were able to defeat satan and take over the old bar at 1241 Blanding Boulevard in Orange Park, Florida. We now have a life-giving church in this building with the Lord's name on it.

However, it was not without warfare done in prayer, intercession, and God dispatching the angel armies to come in and fight on our behalf. Many times, we needed an "angel turnaround." What is an angel turnaround? Angels can actually turn around something bad in our lives that has a barrier or that's not right or that in your eyes is bad or unfruitful, into something good. They actually are sent by God to turn it around and make it into something lovely.

You see, Heaven's job is to protect us, watch over us, and bring down the will of God to earth. God uses His angel messengers to do that because we're His kids and He loves us so much; He wants to make sure that we are protected and taken care of. More than anything, He wants to make sure that His will and purpose, which are always good, will come to pass. He sends angel messengers to planet Earth to help us and to support us. Many times they're placed in situations where God gives them a message to turn around a situation for us.

In this chapter, I share with you quite a few cases in Scripture where God actually sent an angel to turn situations around from bad to good.

In Hebrews, the Word says, *"Are not all angels ministering spirits sent to serve those who will inherit salvation?"* (Heb. 1:14). So, who is to inherit salvation? You and me, all human beings on earth. Angels don't have to be saved, but we have to be saved. We have to come to that place of knowing Jesus Christ as our Lord and Savior; and when we accept Jesus, the One who died on the Cross for us and has forgiven us of our sins having shed His blood for us, then we are considered to be saved.

Angels are ministering spirits sent by God on our behalf so that we might accomplish the plans and purposes of God (see Heb. 1:14). That's what the Word says. We're actually considered to be higher than the angels. Angels protect those who respect God and the will of God, and we know that from the Word, *"The angel of the Lord encamps around those who fear him..."* (Ps. 34:7). God will surely deliver those who respect and revere Him.

That word "angel" in the Hebrew is the word *malak,* which means to dispatch as a deputy, a messenger or one who carries a message. It's almost like a prophet or teacher. It's one who is sent. It's one who is commissioned to perform a purpose for God; God uses angels to accomplish His purposes. He doesn't just use you. You may think the whole world rests on you, but it doesn't. God uses you and angels to accomplish His purpose.

The word "encamps" in the Hebrew is *chanah,* which means to pitch a tent, to abide, to set siege or to watch. When the Word of God says that the angel of the Lord *"encamps around,"* it means that the angel of the Lord abides with us, sets siege with us, watches with us. Connected to that is also the Hebrew word *chanan*, which means to favor us, to have mercy, or to make lovely. Angels are messengers or sent ones that hover over us, protecting our borders and watching to make things lovely for us.

When you are in the worst of times and circumstances, God will send an angel to you to turn around your situation. Later in this chapter, I share with you stories in the Word of God of two courageous men and the angels who were sent to them specifically to turn around their bad situation. If you're declaring and decreeing properly, then you're empowering angels, and you're empowering Heaven. Look at it this way, instead of complaining, grumbling, and murmuring about your situation, if you declare truth, in that moment you will have an angel right there ready to be sent out to the place to support you whatever the situation is.

When you're grumbling, complaining, and moaning, it actually moves earth, but not in a positive way. All that negativity moves earth negatively, but it does not move Heaven to help you positively or accomplish Kingdom purpose. If you want to change something in your life, you have to declare and decree Heaven to change it. You can't move earth to make a positive change, but Heaven will move to affect earth when you ask for help from God. You have to know how the system works. You can most assuredly have heavenly encounters that create supernatural environments.

WE PARTICIPATE WITH ANGELS

When we declare and decree truth, the truth of Heaven, in that moment, angels become activated to turn a situation around. You need to learn how to create a heavenly encounter by calling on the messengers God gave you by declaring the Word of God, declaring truth, declaring what Heaven has said about the situation—then the angels come onboard and interject holiness and righteousness, which turns the situation around for your benefit.

Even this week, I was in intensive prayer for someone and for their destiny. I went into prayer, and I was praying in tongues for hours. I became so entrenched with this particular person and this situation that as I was praying, the Holy Spirit said to me, "The heavens decree and declare a scroll is written over the destiny for this person. I need you to agree with Me that this will come to pass for this person. Will you stand in the gap and declare and decree what Heaven has said? If you do this, I will break it."

I responded, "God, yes I will." As bad as the person's situation was, as soon as I heard from Heaven what Heaven had declared over this person's life, I began to say it over and over again. I noticed a change in the person's life in about 24 hours. What had looked like a completely insurmountable situation, within 24 hours the person was living out the destiny that Heaven had declared. There needed to be someone whom God could put pressure on, an intercessor, to intercede, go into the courts of Heaven, and proclaim fulfillment of the scrolls of Heaven that were written about the person.

Many times when we live with family members or we're around people we know really well and we see the things they do that aren't right or their personality is aggravating, we unfortunately capitulate and end up condoning their acts; we take on an earthly perspective. But God is saying, "Will you declare and decree what *Heaven* has said about them? If you do this, then it will come to pass." A destiny has been written about them. Sometimes we are more concerned about our little argument or what they're doing rather than looking to the declaration that Heaven has made about them. "If you do this, then I will bring it to pass."

This declaration will happen. God needs somebody to do it, somebody to say, "Listen, I know this person's a pain or in pain, but I'm going to make sure that I declare and decree Heaven over this person so I can be of help in creating an atmosphere of Heaven around him or her." This is hard to do in the moment. A lot of the time, the last thing you want to do is declare and decree what Heaven said over people, when you'd really rather be drowning them. Come on, that's truth.

If you can stop for a second and ask God to show you what's been said, just get a glimpse of what Heaven has said, then you can go to that place where they can fulfill their destiny because of you, not because of them, but because you prayed and God sent an angel and the angel turned it around. Because of that, now they're going to step into the destiny that's been written about them from before the foundation of the world was laid.

Let us be these people. Let what I'm saying today motivate you to step into a place where you can help others achieve their God-given destiny. Try it even tonight, especially with the people you don't like, or the person you actually love the most but you don't like at all. Wife, you need to do this for your husband; husband for your wife. Ask God to show you their destiny and begin to intercede for it. See the man or woman God sees, not the crazy person sleeping next to you. Come on, I'm just being honest; you were thinking that. Be someone who declares and decrees for Heaven to step into a person's life so that what Heaven has said about that person will start to be breathed into existence. Ask God what Heaven says about them and then stand in the gap and dispatch angels to make the heavenly change.

Now, let me tell you two stories of two courageous men who persisted while being persecuted. They received persecution for praising God and ministering the Gospel. Both were hunted down by evil people who were not in the will of God. These evil people wanted a throne for themselves, but God sent two courageous men and used them even though they were stuck in incredibly impossible and bad situations. Nonetheless, God sent an angel to help them to be able to come into not only their destiny, but to bring the will of God to pass in others' lives as well.

Let's go to Acts 12 where the Word says:

> *It was about this time that **King Herod arrested some who belonged to the church, intending to persecute them**. He had James, the brother of John, put to death with the sword. When he saw that this met with approval among the Jews, he proceeded to seize Peter also. This happened during the Festival of Unleavened Bread. After arresting him, he put him in prison, handing him over to be guarded by four squads of four soldiers each. Herod intended to bring him out for public trial after the Passover. So **Peter was kept in prison, but the church was earnestly praying to God for him** (Acts 12:1-5).*

THE CHURCH DISPATCHES ANGELIC HOSTS

The Word says that Peter was kept in prison *but* the church was *"earnestly praying to God for him."* Who was praying for him? Hmm... the Church! Guess what, *you* are the Church. When someone gets stuck, you are the *but...the Church* who needs to earnestly pray for that person. What was going to happen after the Passover? Herod was going to bring him to trial. That doesn't happen because God's always on time.

I know we often think God's late, and I know we complain that He's late. I know we complain that He's not listening to us and that He doesn't care. Guess what? Those are lies. He's right on time all the time. I don't always like His timing, but who am I to question God? Sometimes we may think, *God, are You sleeping in? What's going on?* No, He's not asleep; He's right on time, He has already sent the Church to pray:

> *Suddenly an angel of the Lord appeared and a light shone in the cell. He struck Peter on the side and woke him up. "Quick, get up!" he said, and the chains fell off Peter's wrists* (Act 12:7).

God's angel was the turnaround. The situation was bad, but the key to unlocking it was prayer. What was the church doing? Praying. Yes! When you start declaring and decreeing for someone, that's when the angel turnaround happens, that's when Heaven starts moving on the earth to help people get out of bad situations.

> *Then the angel said to him, "Put on your clothes and sandals." And Peter did so. "Wrap your cloak around you and follow me," the angel told him. Peter followed him out of the prison, but he had no idea that what the angel was doing was really happening; he thought he was seeing a vision. They passed the first and second guards and came to the iron gate leading to the city. It opened for them by itself, and they went through it. When they had walked the length of one street, suddenly the angel left him* (Acts 12:8-10).

When this had dawned on him, he went to the house of Mary the mother of John, also called Mark, where many people had gathered and were praying. Peter knocked at the outer entrance, and a servant named Rhoda came to answer the door. When she recognized Peter's voice, she was so overjoyed she ran back without opening it and exclaimed, "Peter is at the door!" "You're out of your mind," they told her. When she kept insisting that it was so, they said, "It must be his angel" (Acts 12:12-15).

I think that is interesting. I mean, an angel released Peter, and then Peter shows up in the flesh at the door and they don't think they see Peter for real. They think they're seeing an angel. Now that's a faith twist. These people had faith, they thought they were seeing angels in the natural. No, it's really Peter in the flesh!

But Peter kept on knocking. When they opened the door and saw him, they were astonished. Peter motioned with his hand for them to be quiet and described how the Lord had brought him out of prison. "Tell James and the other brothers and sisters about this," he said, and then he left for another place. In the morning, there was no small commotion among the soldiers as to what had become of Peter (Acts 12:16-18).

We read, *"there was no small commotion,"* which means there was a *big* commotion among the soldiers as to what had become of Peter. What we see here is that when God decided to send the angel because the Church was praying, and when the angel came on the scene and Peter was released, people's faith increased to a higher level.

People began to be encouraged. What happened to this guy? Where did he go? God showed up on the scene big time when He brought the angel in; but even so, the future looked disastrous for Peter. During our life circumstances, many times that's exactly what God is doing. He wants to show up on the scene and say, "See, I'm here." But because we're so tied up with our little menial problem and our moaning, groaning, and complaining we miss God's presence. Further on in that chapter, we read:

> *On the appointed day Herod, wearing his royal robes, sat on his throne and delivered a public address to the people. They shouted, "This is the voice of a god, not of a man." Immediately, because Herod did not give praise to God, an angel of the Lord struck him down, and he was eaten by worms and died. But the Word of God continued to spread and flourish* (Acts 12:21-24).

Whoa, look what God will do. He will not only send an angel to help you escape your bad situation, He may send one to take care of the enemy. Look at that Scripture passage! They didn't even ask for that to happen. Well, the Word doesn't say whether they were praying for that or not, but I tend to think they were praying for Peter's release. Ultimately, God sent an angel to take care of Herod. Why? Because Herod claimed to be a god himself, and that is something God won't tolerate.

Never try to claim God's name. Herod was claiming to be god with a little g, but nevertheless, Herod was not giving praise to God, so it was time to wipe Herod out. Herod was an enemy. What do we see here? Where prayer is, when people are being persecuted, God will send messengers to help turn the situation around. We need to remember this, because the Church of Jesus Christ is being persecuted even today, not only in our homeland but worldwide. There are horrific stories about believers spreading the Gospel, and the pain and the persecution that they suffer because of it.

ACTIVATE YOUR SPIRITUAL SENSES TO SEE ANGELS

Through the prayers of the Church, God sends angels to do miraculous things. When angels are sent and the miraculous happens, praise must be given to God and the Word of God. Then the Word of God will continue to spread and flourish. You know what, though? God is the same God today as He was back then. He's still sending angels to the scene. Throughout the ages there have been reports of people seeing angels. God sends His angels on assignments to help His children. I've seen angels, and I know many people who have seen them as well. Over the years I've grown to respect them so much more than I did in my early years of being a Christian.

Over the years, I have been growing in this knowledge of angels, and I am so grateful to God for these beautiful creatures that He has sent us—whether we can actually see them or not, we can sense their presence. You too can ask God to give you understanding. Ask the Holy Spirit to give you understanding of sensing the presence of angels. Ask God to activate your spiritual sight so you can discern the presence of angels and participate with them in creating supernatural environments. When we ask God, He will open us up to see what Heaven is doing and what His angels are doing. God will also give you visions of angels and give you dreams. He will enable you to step into that supernatural realm. He wants you to encounter the heavenly dimension so you can create supernatural environments.

As we close out this chapter, let me tell you why it's so important for God that we connect with the heavenly dimension—because the Word says it has to be done on earth as it is in Heaven. If you don't know about your real home, how can you know how to make this place just like that? You can't. You must have some level of understanding about Heaven in order to participate with God to bring Heaven to earth. God wants you to understand.

Heaven is not some far-off paradise place that He doesn't want us to have an understanding about. It's not a place where people sit around doing nothing. They are busy working on the will of God continually. They know about our victories. They know about our defeats. They're up there cheering for us. There is a cloud of witnesses surrounding us, watching what we're doing on a daily basis and giving praise unto God (see Heb. 12:1).

He sends us angels, messengers to help us and come alongside us. There is nothing wrong with praying and declaring and decreeing and asking God to send your angel in to turn things around right now. That should give you some new kind of strength to know that as you pray, God will send His angels to you so you can overcome. We have been called to be overcomers and He sends us heavenly support for this calling!

CHAPTER 12

ANGEL INTERVENTION

I mentioned before that we would not have taken possession of the bar property if it were not for angel intervention. When we were getting ready for our move to the new property, the Lord really helped us make the transition by showing us with seer eyes the angels that were occupying our new facility while we were building it, but also the angels were with us in the sanctuary and all over the building on a daily basis.

We could feel the presence of the angels when the people began to pray. The angels inhabited our prayer circles. They came to listen and obey the instructions we would give to deal with certain situations. Many times, we can sense healing angels and know God wants to do a healing or a miracle. It is then that we do not look at circumstance but keep our eyes on the Spirit and He brings the next move before glory falls.

Our church carries a special torch for revivals and God uses us as a hot spot in our city to pray and intercede for the city. We are daily dispatching angels to do God's work, to go and administer healing, salvation, and deliverance to homes and churches nearby. We also cry out to God to send angels to prepare a way for us much like He did in Exodus 23:20, when He said, *"See, I am sending an angel ahead of you to guard you along the way and to bring you to the place I have prepared."* God will send angels to prepare places and people for a move of God. If revival is to start in people's lives, angels are a key to revival and will begin to stir fire in and around people so they can be revived and help start sparks where God is going. God always has sections of His church people praying for great moves of God, and they require angel intervention.

The angelic hosts are ready to be dispatched on our behalf through our prayers, decrees, and declarations of the Word of God. In a passage in Psalm 91, the Word tells us that:

> *He will command his angels concerning you to guard you in all your ways; they will lift you up in their hands, so that you will not strike your foot against a stone. You will tread on the lion and the cobra; you will trample the great lion and the serpent* (Psalm 91:11-13).

God is waiting for us to ask the angels to move through our prayers to Him and our speaking of the Word of God. In this chapter we discuss two righteous men of God who sought the Lord through prayer. Their lives were a witness to their faith in God and the supernatural to change their devastating circumstances. We too can create supernatural environments through encounters with Heaven that cause us to live by faith and exercise that faith daily!

DON'T RELENT IN YOUR FAITH

Now, let's go to the Book of Daniel. We know from that book, there were some jealous government officials who were absolutely infuriated with Daniel because he was always doing everything right. The Word says that they were administrators and satraps looking for grounds to charge Daniel for his conduct in government affairs. They were unable to condemn Daniel because of his upstanding character. They couldn't find any corruption in him. They couldn't find any basis for charges against him. So what did they have to do? Fabricate and manipulate the scene. They had to figure out a way to get rid of this faithful guy who had great character and had found favor with King Darius.

They went to King Darius and proclaimed, *"May King Darius live forever!"* (Dan. 6:6). Watch out for people who give you a compliment right away, because you don't know what they're ready to do next. After they said, *"May King Darius live forever,"* they turned right around and encouraged King Darius to issue an edict and enforce the decree *"...that anyone who prays to any god or any human being during the next thirty days, except to you, Your Majesty, shall be thrown into the lions' den"* (Dan. 6:6-7). The Word says that:

> *...When Daniel learned that the decree had been published, he went home to his upstairs room where the windows were open toward Jerusalem. Three times a day he got down on his knees and prayed, giving thanks to his God, just as he had done before* (Daniel 6:10).

Read that again, what did Daniel do? He prayed! *"Then these men went as a group and found Daniel praying and asking God for help"* (Dan.6:11).

Well, they thought, there he goes praying to his God. Now we can go back to King Darius and say that Daniel has broken the rule.

As the passage goes on, it says the officials told King Darius that Daniel *"pays no attention to you...he still prays three times a day"* to his

God (Dan. 6:13). *"So the king gave the order, and they brought Daniel and threw him into the lions' den. The king said to Daniel, 'May your God, whom you serve continually, rescue you'"* (Dan. 6:16). That night the Word tells us the king could not sleep. He did not sleep all night long. He enjoyed no entertainment (see Dan. 6:18). He was in distress the entire night, because King Darius really did love Daniel. They had a strong relationship.

The Word doesn't say whether or not King Darius was interceding, but when you have sleepless nights and you don't know where to go, and you don't know what to do, you can bet that his soul was churning something to Heaven during that time about Daniel. Now, this is what happened next:

> *At the first light of dawn, the king got up and hurried to the lions' den. When he came near the den, he called to Daniel in an anguished voice, "Daniel, servant of the living God, has your God, whom you serve continually, been able to rescue you from the lions?" Daniel answered, "May the king live forever! My God sent his angel, and he shut the mouths of the lions. They have not hurt me, because I was found innocent in his sight. Nor have I ever done any wrong before you, Your Majesty." The king was overjoyed and gave orders to lift Daniel out of the den. And when Daniel was lifted from the den, no wound was found on him, because he had trusted in his God. At the king's command, the men who had falsely accused Daniel were brought in and thrown into the lions' den, along with their wives and children (Daniel 6:19-24).*

This is just like the situation that took place with Peter and Herod. It did not work out then and it did not work out here. The plot and plan to kill Daniel did not work because God sent His messenger to the rescue, and there was an angel intervention. The officials who plotted to kill Daniel were thrown into the den along with their wives and children. *"And before they reached the floor of the den, the lions overpowered them and crushed all their bones"* (Dan. 6:24). Not good.

Maybe you ought to find out what side of the game you want to be on before you start playing in it. We know that Daniel was faithful, and he was praying before he was summoned to the den. We know that God heard his faithful prayers. The Word says Daniel prayed three times a day and he did it publicly. He was not afraid of sharing his faith in God with anyone.

BE AUTHENTIC

The Word also says that Daniel was defined as one who was innocent. That word "innocent" means that he was translucent. It means he was authentic. It means there was not a hidden place that had not been exposed. His heart was open. He was a humble man, and he didn't care what anybody said. He was going to do what God wanted him to do. He trusted in God. That's what the Word says. Do you know what that means? It means that Daniel had a character of purity and faithfulness.

Our pure hearts and actions as well as prayer will bring forth an angelic visitation. An angel turnaround and intervention happen not only when we're praying, but also when we're doing the will of God with a faithful and pure heart. Listen, I can tell you right now about hundreds of times when my husband, Pastor Adam, and I have made mistakes. But God has covered them because of His love for us and our character and faithfulness to stand strong in front of Him, including through our prayers. Yes, tons of prayers.

Nobody is perfect and nobody on earth ever will be perfect. Everyone here makes mistakes; but when you know for sure that you have an open heart and an authentic heart before God, He will cover every little mistake that you make. He will turn it around. God will send angels to turn your situation around. He'll make it right, because He knows you can never make anything right on your own. God sees your heart and He hears your prayers, and He says, "I've got to send that faithful one an angel to turn this thing around." We all need angels to intervene for us. What do we have to do? We have to pray and we have to watch our hearts. A broken and contrite heart before God is what He's looking for.

There's a Scripture in Psalm 139 that reads, *"Search me, God, and know my heart; test me and know my anxious thoughts. See if there is any offensive way in me, and lead me in the way everlasting"* (Ps. 139:23-24). We should be praying this prayer all the time. "God, what do You find offensive in me?" When the spirit of offense comes on us, it feels like anger. If you want a good definition of offense, this is it: If you get angry, you're offended. The two go together. Now, you can have righteous anger, there's no doubt about that; but there is also an offense that can come upon you to make you respond in anger.

We have to listen to the anger that rises up in us, and we have to define whether or not we are out of position with that anger, if we have stepped into a place where we are allowing a spirit of offense to rule a situation for us. It will sometimes feel like it is righteous, but I can tell you right now there's less cases of righteous anger than there are of unrighteous anger. If you're going to err on one side or another, take a real good look at yourself when you say you're righteously angry, because there's a very good chance that it's not righteous at all.

Only God determines whether or not it's righteous, because He is the Judge of all. We have to have a heart that says, "God, I'm offended and I'm angry right now, and I'm going to lay my heart before You in all humility and say, 'I don't know if this is righteous or if this is unrighteous. I need You to set this thing straight.'" Whatever it is.

If you lay it down like that, God's going to give you understanding, and He's going to let you know that even if you thought you were fighting a battle for Him and it was a good one, you were way off-base. He will let you know that your battle was not righteous. On the flip side, God may say, "You know what, that is righteous anger and I stand behind you on this one. Let's go ahead and finish this together. I'm going to send an angel to support you on this."

We need to have open hearts before God. When you have that kind of heart, you open yourself up in a brand-new way for angels to intervene in the situation and turn it around. Angel turnarounds do happen. Praying, having a faithful character and purity, and having an authentic heart all open the earthly realm to heavenly intervention and for angelic hosts to come to assist on behalf of the will of God to help His children.

ANGELS TO THE RESCUE

Here is some more relevant truth about God sending angels to the rescue. The prayers of the saints—believers, you and me—send up our needs to God concerning the angels of Heaven, so God can assign the angels to the place of need and fulfill the will of God.

In the Book of Revelation, there were prayers from the saints that went into golden bowls. An angel came and mixed the golden bowls with incense, which means that the angel mixed the prayers of the saints with praise. Then he added in red hot coals from Heaven. Then great things happened (see Rev. 5:8). Now, let's go to Revelation chapter 8. The Word says, *"When he opened the seventh seal, there was silence in heaven for about a half an hour. And I [John] saw seven angels who stood before God and seven trumpets were given to them"* (Rev. 8:1-2).

"Another angel, who had a golden censer, came and stood at the altar. He was given much incense to offer, with the prayers of all God's people...." He was presenting an aroma to God as an offering (see Rev. 8:3). Many times in Scripture incense is burned as an offering to the Lord. Even we are called to be living sacrifices or offerings that are, *"the pleasing aroma of Christ among those who are being saved and those who are perishing"* (2 Cor. 2:15). We are called through Jesus to *"continually offer to God a sacrifice of praise—the fruit of lips that openly profess his name"* (Heb.13:15). So, this incense was a sacrificial offering that brought God praise and adoration.

This angel offered incense, or praise, along with the prayers of all God's people. It's what went in this bowl. On the golden altar in front of the throne, *"the smoke of the incense, together with the prayers of God's people, went up before God from the angel's hand. Then the angel took the censer, filled it with fire from the altar, and hurled it on the earth; and there came peals of thunder, rumblings, flashes of lightning and an earthquake"* (Rev. 8:4-5).

When the Church prays and the prayers of the saints go into bowls in Heaven, and angels come to those bowls with offerings of incense and praise, then a time comes when God will move and release the answers of those prayers of the saints onto the earth. But when does God choose to do that? When the bowls are filled, which are only filled when we pray fervently.

THE ECCLESIA

The *Ecclesia* is a fighting Church, a government set up by God to change environments and to bring dynasty rule or Kingdom rule in a set jurisdiction where God wants to rule. When the *Ecclesia* decides to pray, the prayers go into the bowl and the angel comes forth and touches them with incense, or praise, then God comes and releases the answers to those prayers.

We need to understand that our prayers of intercession are gateways for angelic activity. If you knew how important your prayers were, you would pray a whole lot more than you pray right now. True? You would pray morning, noon, and night! You'd pray without ceasing as Paul says in First Thessalonians 5:16-18. You'd stop fighting everything around you and you'd pray. You'd stop grumbling and complaining and you'd pray. You'd stop being afraid and you'd pray. Fear goes away when Heaven enters the situation. There's no way for faith and fear to reside at the same time, not only in you, but outside you. The same is truth when Heaven comes to invade earth in that space. All fear is gone! This is where we have to look at ourselves.

There are spirits of fear. There's iniquity of fear that rests in people. Maybe you come from a family where fear never goes away, it's something you've always known. You might cover up your fear really well with a lot of good luck and pride. But guess what? God knows it's just a lot of fear. We have to know and understand ourselves. Pride that looks like we know what we're doing when we're really afraid is a false covering for where God intends to work. We need to be continually in prayer (see 1 Thess. 5:17).

We can pray when we are afraid by saying, "God, I'm afraid. God, I don't know how to handle this problem. God, I'm unsure about this issue." You can pray this and at the same time declare what

God wants you to declare so that He can unleash His angelic army to come and turn around what's causing fear inside or outside of you, and bring blessing and light. I want you to agree with God and say, "I'm not going to stop praying. Right here and right now, I'm going to start praying even more than I ever thought possible!"

As the Church, we need to pray more. We need to pray what Heaven says about the situation. Heaven has a beautiful destiny for each of us. Heaven has a beautiful destiny for the moment you're in right now, a beauty that wants to come about even in the midst of your ugly situation. In that instance, Heaven wants to make a resounding exclamation—and it's already been written. All you have to do is ask God to tell you what the situation is supposed to look like, even though that's not what it looks like right now. Begin to declare it and decree it so the angels will be sent to intervene.

What do we need? What does the Church need? An angel turn-around—an angel intervention. How do we cause that to happen? Through prayer, praise, a good character, and open hearts, hearts of authenticity.

VALIANT LEADERSHIP

In Second Chronicles 17, we read about King Jehoshaphat and his favor with the Lord. The Word says:

> **The Lord was with Jehoshaphat** *because he followed the ways of his father David before him. He did not consult the Baals but sought the God of his father and followed his commands rather than the practices of Israel. The Lord established the kingdom under his control; and all Judah brought gifts to Jehoshaphat, so that he had great wealth and honor.* **His heart was devoted to the**

ways of the Lord; *furthermore, he removed the high places and the Asherah poles from Judah* (2 Chronicles 17:3-6).

Jehoshaphat was devoted to God. He prayed and worshipped the Lord. As we read further on in chapter 20 of Second Chronicles, we see that an army was coming to engage Jehoshaphat and his people in a war. But Jehoshaphat was a king who sought the Lord. This is what the Word says about that situation:

> *Alarmed, Jehoshaphat resolved to inquire of the Lord, and he proclaimed a fast for all Judah. The people of Judah came together to seek help from the Lord; indeed, they came from every town in Judah to seek him* (2 Chronicles 20:3-4).

Jehoshaphat proclaimed a fast for all the people that would bring the supernatural into the environment; he prayed and fasted and asked others to do the same. What happens next and what he prays is truly amazing:

> *Then Jehoshaphat stood up in the assembly of Judah and Jerusalem at the temple of the Lord in the front of the new courtyard and said: "Lord, the God of our ances-tors, are you not the God who is in heaven? You rule over all the kingdoms of the nations. Power and might are in your hand, and no one can withstand you. Our God, did you not drive out the inhabitants of this land before your people Israel and give it forever to the descen-dants of Abraham your friend? They have lived in it and have built in it a sanctuary for your Name, saying, 'If calamity comes upon us, whether the sword of judgment,*

or plague or famine, we will stand in your presence before this temple that bears your Name and will cry out to you in our distress, and you will hear us and save us.' But now here are men from Ammon, Moab and Mount Seir, whose territory you would not allow Israel to invade when they came from Egypt; so they turned away from them and did not destroy them. See how they are repaying us by coming to drive us out of the possession you gave us as an inheritance. Our God, will you not judge them? For we have no power to face this vast army that is attacking us. We do not know what to do, but our eyes are on you" (2 Chronicles 20:5-12).

FAITH ACTIVATION

This prayer was so powerful as it was a prayer of submission to the greatness and goodness of God. The people, especially the leaders, were humbling themselves to God and asking for His intervention. Then the Word says a supernatural encounter occurred: *"Then the Spirit of the Lord came on Jahaziel son of Zechariah, the son of Benaiah, the son of Jeiel, the son of Mattaniah, a Levite and descendant of Asaph, as he stood in the assembly"* (2 Chron. 20:14).

This is what Jahaziel prophesies:

Listen, King Jehoshaphat and all who live in Judah and Jerusalem! This is what the Lord says to you: "Do not be afraid or discouraged because of this vast army. For the battle is not yours, but God's. Tomorrow march down against them. They will be climbing up by the Pass of Ziz, and you will find them at the end of the gorge in the Desert of Jeruel. You will not have to fight this battle.

Take up your positions; stand firm and see the deliverance the Lord will give you, Judah and Jerusalem. Do not be afraid; do not be discouraged. Go out to face them tomorrow, and the Lord will be with you" (2 Chronicles 20:15-17).

The first supernatural encounter was having the Spirit of the Lord come upon Jahaziel, but the second supernatural encounter was God fighting the battle for them.

ANGEL AMBUSH

What happened next reveals the real strength of Jehoshaphat's leadership:

Jehoshaphat bowed down with his face to the ground, and all the people of Judah and Jerusalem fell down in worship before the Lord. Then some Levites from the Kohathites and Korahites stood up and praised the Lord, the God of Israel, with a very loud voice (2 Chronicles 20:18-19).

Praise and worship were the response of the people in faith as they believed God was going to fight this battle for them. This is what the Word says happened next:

Jehoshaphat stood and said, "Listen to me, Judah and people of Jerusalem! Have faith in the Lord your God and you will be upheld; have faith in his prophets and you will be successful." After consulting the people, Jehoshaphat appointed men to sing to the Lord and to praise him for the splendor of his holiness as they went out at the head of the army, saying: "Give thanks to the Lord, for his love endures forever" (2 Chronicles 20:20-21).

These folks just kept singing and praising. The more they exalted God, the more He finished the job. The Lord sent armies to ambush the enemy. Was there a supernatural force behind these ambushes? I believe God was giving instructions to the angels as the people prayed and fasted; then angelic hosts were sent in to fight in the spirit realm first, before the effects were witnessed in the natural realm. The Word says:

> *As they began to sing and praise, the Lord set ambushes against the men of Ammon and Moab and Mount Seir who were invading Judah, and they were defeated. The Ammonites and Moabites rose up against the men from Mount Seir to destroy and annihilate them. After they finished slaughtering the men from Seir, they helped to destroy one another* (2 Chronicles 20:22-23).

This battle was won by God! God can do anything to bring us into His purpose. However, in order for this battle to be won, the supernatural had to be activated. This activation came by prayer, fasting, faith, and praise! These are our weapons of warfare and they activate the heavens to respond and sow into the earth.

There is so much to learn in this prayer about seeing a mighty move of God. In a different passage in Second Chronicles, we read about the Lord speaking to King Solomon:

> *When I shut up the heavens so that there is no rain, or command locusts to devour the land or send a plague among my people, if my people, who are called by my name, will humble themselves and pray and seek my face and turn from their wicked ways, then I will hear from*

heaven, and I will forgive their sin and will heal their land (2 Chronicles 7:13-14).

All these Scriptures and truths I have been sharing with you are keys right from the Word of God for opening the heavens to see changes in our environments. When we pray and seek His face together as a community of believers, God comes to move supernaturally to change circumstances for His glory and our good. God will move on our behalf, dispatch angels, and bless us with heavenly encounters when we stay faithful to Him, and are people of integrity, character, and seek God for every need, believing He will release Heaven according to His will.

CHAPTER 13

THE FAITH OF GOD
FOR MIRACLES

When I began to learn about the faith of God and walking in it to see miracles and healings, I had to tune my spiritual senses to tap into the faith God had for a situation. I had to tune my heavenly frequency to God's desire to bless someone. I had to leave behind my agenda and time frame and enter environments saying, "God, You want to accomplish something here; let me surrender." I had to stop looking *around* me and look *internally* to the glory of God inside me. The fullness of His substance within me.

Then as I worshipped Him, automatically I would begin to agree in the supernatural with what God wanted to do—then I just stepped out and He would do it. The training came when I began to listen more and then just do it without first checking whether or not my surroundings would be acceptable to a heavenly encounter.

Instead, I did as God said and ignored the environment altogether. I stopped thinking about appropriateness and started thinking, *I would rather encounter God than be correct in this situation.* Then I made a move of faith and He would meet it. This is how I learned to walk in healing and miracles and still walk that way today. It is a simple faith response for seeing Heaven move in the earthly realm and create a supernatural environment. You see it first in a spirit-to-Spirit connection with Him as you agree in your heart and do it, then He changes the environment.

Queen Esther tapped into the faith of God to free a nation. She believed that God would indeed come to rescue her and the Jewish people and help them escape annihilation by the evil plot of Haman. She did not look at her circumstance, she looked to her God. The story of her life in the Bible shows the power of prayer, fasting, and faith activation. Esther, according to the Word of God, had come to her royal position for *"such a time as this"* (Esther 4:14). She was ordained to be the instrument God would use to save the Jewish people from death. She called for a fast for three days before she went to the king to tell him about the evil plot.

During the corporate prayer and fasting time, Esther's faith was activated along with the faith of others, and God did indeed move on behalf of the nation. If we look at Esther's faith, she's no different from you or me. She was made for a purpose and so are you. She was put in a position where her faith had to be activated in order to go into the presence of the king, as she very well might have lost her life in doing so. This was a life-threatening call for Esther.

Today, many people feel like they are on the brink of life-and-death matters that require the faith of God or a God kind of faith, just like Esther years ago.

In this chapter you will come to understand the importance of tapping into the faith of God, or the God kind of faith, in order to open Heaven so the supernatural can come and impact your natural world. Jesus desires to change environments, but He needs us to believe and act so He can do it.

THE FAITH OF GOD

You need to have faith in order to listen to the voice of God and respond to Him when He tells you to move forward in His plans for your life. In this chapter, I share with you some really intensive truth that will help you make decisions about moving in faith. I share with you the power of the gift of faith and walking in the faith *of* God to encourage supernatural encounters.

In Galatians, the apostle Paul wrote of the faith *of* God:

> *I am crucified with Christ: nevertheless I live; yet not I, but Christ liveth in me: and the life which I now live in the flesh I live by* **the faith of the Son of God**, *who loved me, and gave himself for me. I do not frustrate the grace of God: for if righteousness come by the law, then Christ is dead in vain* (Galatians 2:20 KJV).

We know the apostle Paul went through tremendous trials, temptation, imprisonment, flogging, and many other types of public persecutions, and he writes it was the faith *of* the Son of God that helped him get through all of it. That is the kind of faith we need to have. You might ask, "Okay, well how does the faith *of* God work?" This is supernatural. When you grasp this understanding, this is going to forever change how you operate in the realms of faith.

The faith *of* God means you attach to God in a way that you're believing Him for what He already believes for you. God believes in and for you, and you must tap into what He already believes for you.

See, that's different from just saying, "I need to believe in this," or, "I need to see this happen." What you really need to tap into is the fact that God's belief for you is what you need to believe in too. Then you will see it happen in your life! I can tell things are shifting right now in your brain.

When we tap into the faith that God has for us in a particular situation or environment, then we tap into making the impossible possible. Without faith, it is impossible to please God, but we must believe that He exists and is the rewarder of those who seek Him (see Heb. 11:6).

We know that when faith is active the way God wants it to be, the impossible becomes possible. So, let me take you to some real practical Scriptures. In Luke 5, Jesus is standing by the Lake of Gennesaret, meaning the Sea of Galilee. The people are crowding around Him, and they're listening to the Word of God. They're what? They're listening to the Word of God. Faith comes by hearing and hearing by the Word of God (see Rom. 10:17).

When you hear the Word of God, your faith begins to increase. When you're sitting in an environment where you're hearing the Word of God, your faith increases. You can even read the Word of God to yourself and your faith will increase. If you read the Word out loud to yourself that is even better because not only do you take it into your mind, but also into your ears. These folks were listening to the Word of God and then Jesus got into one of the boats, the one belonging to Simon, and He asked Simon Peter to put out a little from the shore. "Hey, Simon. Take Me out a little bit."

Then Jesus sat down and taught the people from the boat. Jesus is teaching the people (Luke 5:3). Why? So their faith would increase. He's setting a supernatural atmosphere for something to happen here.

Faith first comes by Him speaking the Word to the people. He's talking, so His preaching increases faith. He is the Word of God in action. We know this from John, *"The Word became flesh and made His dwelling among us. We have seen his glory, the glory of the one and only Son, who came from the Father, full of grace and truth"* (John 1:14). They were exposed to the Word of God in the flesh in Jesus Christ and also the Word of God as it was spoken. Today we have the Word of God that is alive and active, and is life to the spirit, soul, and body; and when it is read, it brings forth supernatural power (see Heb. 4:12).

"When he [Jesus] had finished speaking, he said to Simon, 'Put out into deep water and let down the nets for a catch'" (Luke 5:4). Jesus sets the framework of presenting the Gospel and speaking it. He's speaking the Word, and it increases the faith of all who hear Him. Then He tells the disciples exactly what to do, now that their faith is increased. *"Simon answered, 'Master, we've worked hard all night and haven't caught anything. But because you say so, I will let down the nets'"* (Luke 5:5).

In other words, Simon Peter is responding exactly how we respond, "God, don't You know that You were late yesterday and now I'm wrestling with major fear and doubt right now? Why are You telling me to do that? I'm not interested in doing that." Or, "God, don't You know I already tried that yesterday, the week before, last month, last year, two years ago, and nothing happened? Why are You asking me to do that again?" He sets the stage. He preaches the Word. He tells the guys, *"Let down the nets."*

One of them comes back and says something like, "Uh, why should I do that? I already fished all night. It's not working. But, yea, I'll try again." So, he does and the Word says, *"When they had done so, they caught such a large number of fish that their nets began to break"*

(Luke 5:6). These guys obeyed Jesus despite their prior disappointments and doubts, and then their nets began to break because there were so many fish. They signaled their partners in the other boat to come and help them, and they came and filled both boats so full of fish that they began to sink (Luke 5:7).

FAITH OVERRULES FEAR AND DOUBT

Now let's recap what we have learned. When the Word is spoken, our faith is increased. Faith meets a person or a group of people who say, "Don't you know I've already done that? But I'll try it again." "I'll try again" means that the faith of Simon Peter and the crew caused them to obey—even though in the natural they didn't think they would catch anything. They surrendered to the Word being spoken by the Word, which was Jesus. If God tells us to do something, that means it's going to happen, and so Simon Peter and the other disciples had to agree that what God said was indeed going to happen. Once they did that, they put their obedience into action.

Now, they might have only had a little faith for they had been in doubt, but nonetheless, they had to have the faith *of* God to believe the Word that was said by Jesus enough to cast the net. Then the miracle happened. God blessed them. That must have been amazing to see the miraculous load of fish that was so big they had to ask their partners to come help. I don't know about you, but I would like to see a miracle so extravagant that I could not manage it without help. That is when you know the impossible has happened—when the load is so overwhelming and huge that you need to restructure everything about your life to accommodate it.

Now the miracle continues because after Simon Peter sees the miracle, he falls at Jesus' knees and says, *"Go away from me, Lord; I am a sinful man!"* (Luke 5:8). This same thing happens to us when we see God do a mighty work in our lives. We get on our knees and say, "My God, how did I doubt You? What a sinner I am! You came through and I actually didn't think You were going to." The grace of God will cause our hearts to repent of not believing Him, and not having the faith that He has for the situations we are faced with.

This very similar story is recorded in John chapter 21 after Jesus is resurrected. The guys are fishing all night. Jesus again, from the shoreline says, "Hey, have you caught any fish?" Now, how would you react if you've been up all night and you caught nothing? "No, thanks for reminding me. No, we got nothing, pal." But it's Jesus talking and He says, *"Throw your net on the right side of the boat and you will find some"* (John 21:5-6).

FAITH OF GOD PRODUCES MIRACLES

These stories about the faith *of* God in Luke 5 and John 21 are almost parallel. When you align yourself with the faith *of* God, or the *God kind of faith*, it will sink the current capacity of your life with blessings. Your boat cannot *not* handle the blessings God puts on it if you have the *God kind of faith*. This is the kind of faith we need to be asking God for daily! "God, please give me the God kind of faith where You are ready to do a miracle and I am only to join You there with faith and action to see it happen."

Now please know that it's okay if you're lacking some faith and belief. After all, these guys were with Jesus for three and a half years, and saw miracles multiple times, yet they still didn't get it. Right around the corner, God is waiting for you to have the God kind of faith, and He's going to sink the current capacity of what you're doing. In other words, He's going to bless you so much that you will have to expand your mindset to accept it all. That's what you need to hear.

Again, returning to Luke chapter 5, Simon Peter is repenting because He saw the goodness of God in this miracle. Anytime we see the miracles of God, we become overwhelmed with self-doubt, fear, and self-condemnation for doubting Him. Jesus tells Simon there's no need to be ashamed or fearful. Jesus says, *"Don't be afraid; from now on you will fish for people"* (Luke 5:10). In other words, in that moment doubt was overcome by the faith connection between Simon and Jesus. And after he repents, Jesus gives him an assignment for his destiny.

Likewise, your destiny is right before you and God is promising big things; but you must first ask Him for the faith of God for this destiny. You have to believe what God believes for the situation, because that's when the miracles happen, that's when a blessing so great will come into your life that you won't know what to do with it.

THE WOMAN WITH THE ISSUE OF BLOOD

The second story I want to share about the faith of God is seen in a passage in Matthew:

> *Just then a woman who had been subject to bleeding for twelve years came up behind him and touched the edge of his cloak. She said to herself, "If I only touch his cloak, I will be healed"* (Matthew 9:20-21).

The part of Jesus' cloak that the woman touched is called the tzitzit, part of His prayer shawl. That's another sermon for another time. When she touches the cloak, she says she will be healed. Then Jesus turns to her and says, *"Take heart, daughter…your faith has healed you.' And the woman was healed at that moment"* (Matt. 9:22).

Now, what does this mean about the faith *of* God for seeing miracles happen? The same event is recorded in Luke 8:43-47. Luke, a disciple of Christ who was by profession a doctor, tells the story from the standpoint where Jesus says, *"Who touched me?"* (Luke 8:45). There was so much power created between the attachment of this woman's faith and the faith that Jesus Himself had to heal anybody at any time. When Jesus walks, no matter where He walks, He walks already with the intention of bringing healing at any moment. He walks into every environment already knowing that there's an expectation of a need that has to be met by someone and that He is the One in authority to meet that need. As He walks into any situation, it is already there in His being that if someone's faith is activated, a miracle is going to happen.

DETERMINE TO BELIEVE

The Word tells us in that passage that when the woman touched His garment while He was walking through the crowd, that many other people were touching Him too. So it begs the question, why was she the only one healed? The Word says, *"She said to herself, 'If I only touch his cloak, I will be healed'"* (Matt. 9:21). This means she determined in her mind before even approaching Jesus that she would be healed by only touching His clothes.

Now, this is really, really important. She believed that if she could touch Him, she would be healed. Now how did she come up with that? The faith of God was deposited inside her that when she came near Him she would be healed. That was a prior action on her part before she ever came close to touching Him. She received the gift of faith from God Himself and believed in her soul. She had met with God already in her heart. "I believe already if I touch Him that I will be healed" (see Matt. 9:21). You have to agree with God that if He wants to do something in your life, He will indeed do it. You and God make the agreement, and then when He shows up, your faith attaches with His faith, and boom, there's electricity and it happens.

The word "touched" in the Greek translates to the word *hapto-mai,* which means to properly attach oneself. But this can also be broken down further in the Greek language to the word *hapto,* which means to fasten, as in to set on fire. So, to quickly recap, when the Word says that the woman touched Jesus, that actually means that fire came through an attachment that made a difference in her life.

To the Jewish people this woman was unclean, an impure woman because she had been bleeding all those years. No one wanted to touch her. Jesus was pure in every regard. Jesus kept the entire Torah. There was no law He ever broke. He was holy. He was righteous. He was a lover of people regardless of whether or not they were impure. He loved first in everything He did and wanted people to know this truth. This woman knew in her heart she would not be cast out by Him, that He would love her and meet her need despite her impurity of blood.

When Jesus entered a situation, He knew that if somebody's faith attached with His faith, then boom, a miracle was going to happen. She believed in the character of God to love her and His desire to heal her. This was enough to activate the faith of God in her and touch Jesus' heart.

AGREE WITH GOD'S DESIRES

Now let's go back to the disciples in the Luke 5 and John 21. Jesus had to activate their faith to match His faith. Jesus was already there, wanting to do a miracle to make the fish go into those nets so that they would have more than they ever imagined. He was ready for a miracle, and He coaxed them through discussion to respond to His faith even in their state of fear and doubt.

Do you understand what I'm saying? God will, if necessary, drag you into the place with Him where you have your fears and doubts. But in that place, He will position you for the blessing that He wants to give you. God will even say, "Will you agree with Me? Come on. If you just do this. Just do this one thing." All that He's saying is, "Get out of that rut, get out of that place, and position yourself because I'm about to do a miracle in this house tonight." We have to realize that everywhere He is, He walks with the expectation that someone will be healed, someone will be delivered, someone will be saved.

Many times, through all the miracles that He does, He just wants to know if there's someone expecting a miracle in this place. Maybe you are asking God, "I just want to be saved, healed, delivered. I want my spouse to be saved, healed, delivered. I want my family to be right with God. I want financial blessing." If you're asking God for that, let your faith attach with His faith, and He will do the miracle in your life.

Now if you're challenged by this word, you should be challenged enough to ask God, "How can I have the faith *of* God, the *God kind of faith*, where I'm going to begin to see miracles happen in my life? How can I change my thinking? God, if You're always ready to do something, why don't I get that about You? I'm not attaching with You like the woman who touched Your garment."

He definitely is ready to do something. But are you ready to believe that He will? If you're doubtful, it's okay. Peter questioned. He had doubts, but Jesus coaxed him into the place of blessing, so I'm going to challenge you. If you're sitting in fear and doubt, if you're sitting in worry and discouragement, if you're sitting in a place where you're not sure if God is going to do it because maybe you've asked and it hasn't happened yet, or maybe it goes year after year after year with no miracle—it's time to say, "God, give me the God kind *of* faith that I need to have so *I* can believe what *You* believe for my situation."

The Word says in Matthew 5:8, *"Blessed are the pure in heart, for they will see God."* That word "heart" translates to *kardia* in the Greek language, and it means that your mind, your feelings, your emotions are pure. When we have fear, doubt, worry, and we're always questioning, we're impure of heart. We're not going to see God work. You need to increase your faith. Simon Peter was in that place: "Jesus, don't You know? I've been throwing these nets over all night long. Where have You been?" Jesus says, "Enough with you. I preached the Word of God. Faith is increased in this house." What is Jesus saying? "I preached the Word to the people. Faith is increased. Simon, I'm telling you, put those nets over the side." Simon Peter acquiesces and finally does what he's told to do by Jesus (see Luke 5:5).

Maybe at this point in your faith walk, you do come with that attitude, okay—but still do what Jesus tells you to do. Do the crazy thing. That was crazy to the fishermen because they had been up all night fishing and caught nothing. Then repentance came and then salvation came. So much more came. A new assignment came for Peter as a result of what? Obedience. As a result of attaching his faith to God coaxing him to have enough faith to get himself set up to be a fisher of people, not just a fisher of fish that someone was going to eat.

The dream inside you is big, and it takes faith to make it a reality. The only way you're going to get there is if you activate your faith with God in the place where He's calling you to activate it. Let me tell you, that's a whole other message, but do you understand? If God says, "I'm moving you right now," you need to have the faith of God, and your question for Him needs to be, "God, give me Your God kind *of* faith. I don't have it yet."

Right now I would like you to do an important exercise. Simply write down what you're not believing God for; in other words, write down your doubts and fears. Then ask Him to give you the faith to believe what He wants to give you in this effort. This is what I believe— your faith will increase, especially if you get into the Word of God and you start believing the Scriptures that say the impossible is possible.

You have to wash yourself with the Word of God (see Eph. 5:26). You must open your ears and listen to it. Faith comes by hearing and hearing by the Word of God. You need to say the Word over and over again so it's louder than the voice in your head and louder than the demonic forces telling you your dream is not going to happen. That's the God kind *of* faith you have to have if you want to see a God kind *of* faith miracle. And God intends to give you a God kind *of* faith miracle because throughout His Word, He proves that when His faith and the faith of somebody else connects, boom, it happened.

Maybe you need to commit to living for Jesus again in your life. Maybe you need a healing. Maybe God is saying, "Touch the hem of My garment for physical, mental, emotional healing, spiritual healing." Whatever it is, you just need to ask God for His faith so you can believe what He wants to do. Ask and you shall receive!

CHAPTER 14

JESUS IS WILLING TO HEAL

In 2004, I suffered from intense pain down the left side of my body—it went from my head all the way down my arm. Many times, I wondered whether or not I was having a stroke because it was so severe. Each time I felt the pain, I would do all I could to ignore it and not fear. I would recite Scriptures to myself about the fact that God had a purpose and destiny for me and that I would not die, but I was going to live and God would carry out His plan.

One day I asked the pastor of my church to pray for me and anoint me with oil. He said he would pray for me but his church did not believe in anointing with oil for healing. I was like, *What?* Then please explain this Scripture in the Book of James:

> *Is anyone among you sick? Let them call the elders of the church to pray over them and anoint them with oil in the name of the Lord. And the prayer offered in faith will make the sick person well; the Lord will raise them up. If they have sinned, they will be forgiven* (James 5:14-15).

God had given me the faith to ask for prayer as well as anointing with oil, but my pastor would not do it. I was confused. I went home and said, "Lord, what is this? You tell me to go to my pastor and have him lay hands on me and anoint me with oil and he says he can only do part of Your Word?" This is bogus, this does not sound right. Then I heard the Lord say to me, "Call the church down the street, they will lay hands on you and anoint you with oil and the prayer of faith will heal you!" I called my husband and told him and he said, yes, go down the street. So, I called them and they said, "Come over now, the two pastors and the church secretary will pray for you!" So, I did.

These three people began to pray for me and lay hands on my arm and neck and anointed me with oil—and I was healed! No more pain ever came back in my arm or neck. It was truly the faith of God in action. God told me to go and that was His will to heal me. I knew it was His will from the Word because He is the Healer. I was touched with a special gift of faith. I knew I would be healed if I was prayed for and anointed with oil in accordance with the Word of God, and no one could tell me otherwise. God told me what to do even with the blockade from my church pastor, and I was healed doing it His way.

Needless to say, we left that church. My husband and I were teachers there, so that had made it difficult, but we knew we could no longer stay. We decided to attend the church down the street, which opened up tons of heavenly encounters for us. That is where my husband received the baptism of the Holy Spirit; and during that time, I began my radio and television ministry and had my first encounter being caught up to Heaven. This began my journey of creating supernatural environments with heavenly encounters. God knows what He is doing. He will take sick people and make them voices for His glory!

FAITH LEADS TO GRACE

In the last chapter we talked about walking in the faith *of* the Son of God. I discussed how the apostle Paul wrote of this in Galatians:

> *I am crucified with Christ: nevertheless I live; yet not I, but Christ liveth in me: and the life which I now live in the flesh I live by the faith of the Son of God, who loved me, and gave himself for me. I do not frustrate the grace of God: for if righteousness come by the law, then Christ is dead in vain* (Galatians 2:20-21 KJV).

Now, what Paul is saying here is that he has the faith of the Son of God. So not only does he have faith *in* the Son of God and what Christ has done for him on the Cross, but he actually, literally has the faith *of* God for the situations in his life. We know that righteousness comes by faith (see Rom. 4:13). In other words, God considers you to be a righteous person if you have faith. It's not whether or not you've done all things right according to the law, it's about your faith. We have established that faith is a key aspect to seeing anything move in the supernatural realm.

When we have faith, then we don't frustrate the grace of God. God's grace can begin to move freely in and around our lives when we meet Him with faith. When we receive an understanding of what God wants to do, and when we can agree with God on that, then we will begin to live by the agreement we have with God.

Romans 5:1-2 says, *"Therefore, since we have been justified through faith, we have peace with God through our Lord Jesus Christ, through whom we have gained access by faith into this grace in which we now stand...."* The grace of God is necessary for miracles and healing, and so is understanding the authority of Christ over the supernatural realm.

When you recognize the fact that Christ has authority over all things in your life, and that God gave Him that authority, and He is giving that to you through the power of the Holy Spirit, then you can submit yourself to His authority that is part of the activation of your faith. Again, Paul says, *"The life which I now live in the flesh I live by the faith of the Son of God, who loved me, and gave himself for me"* (Gal. 2:20 KJV). In other words, he says, "I recognize my death, burial, and resurrection in Christ, and although I'm walking in this body, I am interconnected in union with Him. I have the faith of the Son of God."

When God says believe it, I attach myself to that faith in Him and then I step out. In stepping out I do not frustrate the grace of God, rather the grace of God then begins to move in my life. I begin to see miracles happen because I begin to connect with the faith of God. The apostle Paul writes, *"I do not frustrate the grace of God: for if righteousness come by the law, then Christ is dead in vain"* (Gal. 2:21 KJV). In other words, if righteousness came by the law, or just by what *Paul* did, then that would be frustrating the grace of God. He says he is righteous by faith.

Therefore, so are we as believers, and we get to receive all the things that come by faith as a free gift of grace through our death, burial, and resurrection in Christ, which is why Jesus did not die in vain. The disciples knew this and they saw miracles happen because of the faith that God stretched in the lives of His disciples. Matthew 8:1-3 says:

> When Jesus came down from the mountainside, large crowds followed him. A man with leprosy came and knelt before him and said, "Lord, if you are willing, you can make me clean." Jesus reached out his hand and touched the man. "I am willing," he said. "Be clean!" Immediately he was cleansed of his leprosy.

JESUS IS WILLING TO DO MIRACLES

Now, let's break down these Scripture verses. The interesting thing is that this man knelt before Jesus and said, *"Lord, if you are willing, you can make me clean."* Now, let's get this straight. If Jesus is right in front of you, is He not willing to heal you? Now see, that depends upon your faith. Do you believe in the character and the nature of God? Do you believe that He loves you? Do you believe that He is the Healer? Do you believe that He is the Provider? Do you believe that it is His desire to see you healed and whole and delivered? If you believe these statements are true about Jesus, why would you ask, "*if you're willing?*" You would not ask that question. Yet this man asked that question. Now what can we learn from this? Jesus' response to the question was to reach out his hand and touch the man and say, *"I am willing. Be clean!"* (Matt. 8:3).

His response to the man reveals the nature of God—He is willing. The great I Am is willing to heal you. He is willing to do a miracle in your life. He is willing to meet you where you are and answer the prayers you have been praying. He is willing to do this. That word "willing" in its Greek form is *thelo*, which actually means to delight in, to love, to determine, an impulse. Basically, Jesus is saying, "I am willing as I delight in you. I love you. I am determined. I move on impulse." That's His response.

But let's go one step deeper, because that Greek word is also founded on another Greek root word *aihreomai*. This word supports *thelo* and means to delight in and to love. It also means to take for oneself or to choose. In other words, Jesus is saying, "I choose to take you for myself and to delight in and love you."

Now let's go one step deeper in that Greek word, which is *ahero*. It means to expiate sin or to lift up, loose, elevate, or remove. It is the same word we see when it comes to having confidence in Christ and understanding that when He died on the Cross, was buried, and resurrected, He expiated your sin. He atoned for your sin so that you may have life and live it to its full abundance. He got rid of obstacles in your life to move forward in your destiny. He took care of that for you. Therefore, the lowest level of this word is the word to make you whole and to make you clean. It's a word that says, "I lifted you up. I have done the work for you already, and I choose to take you for myself and delight in and love you. I am determined and compelled to do this." That's the totality of word *thelo* when He says He's "willing."

Jesus died on the Cross for you, was buried, and resurrected so you can receive the Holy Spirit and have all of His power inside you to live your life and live it to a greater fullness of abundancy. Therefore, you have the fullness of God in you because He is willing. He was willing to go the Cross for you, to cleanse you of your sins—not only that, but He is also willing to do miracles in your life as well! His willingness doesn't stop when you are saved. His willingness goes to the level of making you whole in every area of your life, and positioning you for abundant life.

There's another key in Matthew to discuss. Jesus was talking to the disciples and says, *"...if you have faith and do not doubt, you will not only do what was done to the fig tree, but also if you say to this mountain, 'Be removed and be cast into the sea,' it will be done"* (Matt. 21:21 NKJV). That word "removed" is the same Greek word *ahero,* as used in Matthew 8:3, which means if you do not doubt you can speak it and it shall happen. In other words, you can say to the mountain be removed and it will be removed or be gone. This is just like saying Jesus Christ takes away our sin because "removed" is the same Greek word *ahero.*

Here is the key, if you say to this mountain, be removed—in other words, obstacle be gone with you, which takes much of your faith to do so—what you're putting into action is what has already been done for you. You are putting into action by faith the power of Christ's death, burial, and resurrection and now you are coming to a place where you can articulate it out of your mouth and say *be removed* and the obstacle is cast into the sea just as your sin was removed. I have agreed with God and I'm stepping into the place that He's called me to be. This place was accomplished already on the cross so I can walk in the fullness now. Things can be removed in my life that are obstacles. This is a place of faith miracles. You are stepping into the power of *ahero* in that He delights in you and loves you and is willing to move mountains for you.

AUTHORITY FOR MIRACLES

Now, let's talk about authority and how it works in the case of faith activation and seeing miracles happen in our environments because of heavenly encounters. In Matthew 8:5-10, we see the case of the centurion. This is what the Word says took place:

And when Jesus had entered Capernaum, a centurion came to Him, pleading with Him, saying, "Lord, my servant is lying at home paralyzed, dreadfully tormented." And Jesus said to him, "I will come and heal him" (Matthew 8:5-7 NKJV).

So, when the centurion comes, he says, listen my servant's at home paralyzed, suffering. Jesus says, *"I will come and heal him."* That's Jesus' response. But the centurion responds:

"Lord, I am not worthy that You should come under my roof. But only speak a word, and my servant will be healed. For I also am a man under authority, having soldiers under me. And I say to this one, 'Go,' and he goes; and to another, 'Come,' and he comes; and to my servant, 'Do this,' and he does it." When Jesus heard it, He marveled, and said to those who followed, "Assuredly, I say to you, I have not found such great faith, not even in Israel!" (Matthew 8:8-10 NKJV)

Now let's talk about this centurion's faith connected with Jesus. The centurion comes to Him telling Him about his servant, and Jesus does what? He responds as one "willing." "I'm willing to come." The first time they meet, Jesus is willing. This is another case from Scripture where Jesus is willing.

What are you learning about the heart of God here? He is willing to do these things in your life. He is willing and He is ready and He has heard your prayer and He intends to respond.

The problem happens when we don't agree with God about who God is in a moment. The enemy is sure to convince us that God is not coming to our rescue, that God has not heard our prayer, that

God does not care, that God is not moving something, or anything at all. The enemy puts us in a state of fear and doubt. Our human nature is attracted to fear and doubt. Why? Because when Adam and Eve sinned in the Garden, that became our first nature. But that is not our second nature. Our second nature is that we are born again, baptized in the Holy Spirit, and that Jesus is willing. He is willing from the time before we even know Him to when we do know Him. But we have to be mature Christians and start to step into a place of saying, "Jesus is willing." Can you say out loud right now, "Jesus is willing!"

We have to increase our faith. When Jesus says, "I am willing to heal him," the centurion tells Jesus, "You don't need to come to my house here." This statement of belief reveals the centurion's faith. Now the centurion is logically stating the facts, because as a soldier he knows that when he makes a command, his subordinates respond. He sees Jesus as a commander, and he's saying if Jesus says the word, it will happen.

But let me tell you what happened deeper, underneath the surface of this dialogue. Jesus and the centurion, although the centurion is relating it to natural means of authority, have come into a place of agreement. They have begun to agree. The faith of the centurion was so strong that he and Jesus agreed at that moment that the servant should be healed!

See, it's more than the fact that the centurion had a logical understanding of leadership and was a commander and knew how it worked. He just put the natural into play. But the truth of the matter is that his faith was so strong that Jesus answered. Think of it like this, "This is where my faith is, just say the word and it will be done." And Jesus said okay.

Now, we have to look at our own faith. We need to recognize Jesus as the authority in every situation in our life. Whether or not you've ever been in a situation where you truly understood natural authority like the centurion did, you have to understand God's system of authority and rulership—Jesus is at the top of the food chain. If Jesus says it shall be done, it shall be done.

Now half of the problem with us is that we're not sure Jesus said, "It shall be done." This is where most of our problems lie in the area of faith. We question if it really will be done. We question whether or not Jesus is going to do the impossible. We always question, and God is trying to get us to a place of agreeing with Him; if He said it, we should agree with Him that it shall be done.

I'm looking for that kind of faith. Does anybody understand what kind of faith that is? There are some people who push themselves to operate at that level. You can shift your mind right now and get to the place where you start agreeing with God about what God is saying about you and your circumstance. You can shift your mind where you can begin to see miracles happen around you. Why? Because He is there and He wants to do something for you. You just have to believe that is true. You have to change your thinking. When you are there, it's not just you there—Jesus is there too. Who's sitting next to you? Jesus. If Jesus is in the room, what does He want to do? Heal, deliver, save, restore, redeem. When Jesus is here, He wants to do something. Open yourself to Him.

JESUS INTENDS TO HEAL

Now I'm going to teach you something about the power of healing and the power of prophecy, and you can take this anywhere if you allow it to sink into your spirit. Wherever you are—whether at home, your job, in the supermarket, if you believe Jesus is there, then He wants to do something. Just ask Him, "Jesus, what do You want to do in this place right now?" When you have an open heart of faith like that, it's because you understand He's with you, and He has come to do something. Then He will begin to speak to you about what it is He wants to do.

But why will He speak to you? Because He wants to do a healing in this place right now. So many times, our thoughts are self-centered, including focusing on our sins or the mistakes that we make. But Jesus took care of all that by His death, burial, and resurrection. He just wants you on board with Him to be a vessel to advance the Kingdom of God. Jesus' thoughts are on moving forward and our thoughts many times are on ourselves. We need to be God-minded and think about what is important to Jesus first. Then we open ourselves up to tap into the faith realm and see miracles happen.

There are so few people who see healing and miracles because they're so consumed with their own issues and not willing to believe that Jesus is here and wants to do something. Now let's go to the next level of thinking. When you're at home, at your job, or anywhere, there is always someone who's been praying. You don't know what they've been praying, and you won't have a clue unless the Holy Spirit tells you.

In all of the scriptural examples we've discussed, someone had a need. In the last chapter, we talked about the woman with the issue of blood who touched the hem of Jesus' garment. That was so powerful because for twelve years she was hemorrhaging. The number 12 is the number of governmental authority; so for twelve years, until she touched governmental authority, she carried this issue with her. She had been praying for twelve years. Did God not hear that prayer for all those years? Of course, He did.

But when Jesus was there and she was there, an amazing thing happened. All of that praying had raised her to a higher level of faith so that when she and Jesus were in the same vicinity, Jesus was ready to do a miracle for her even though He didn't know she was there until she touched Him. Why? Because in the supernatural, her prayer had already been answered. She just had to meet Jesus. Now, you are that person walking around with authority, who knows Jesus, and needs to ask God, "Somebody's praying in this place. What is it that they're asking You for?"

When the prayer goes up, He's already got the answer. And if you're tuned in, you're going to be able to address that issue. Not because of you, but because you're going to invite Jesus to be who He wants to be in that person's life, and you are the one who listened. We're all at different levels of spiritual maturity; some people aren't even aware that they have the power of Holy Spirit to tap into that place with God. That they can be used of Him to open the door to deliverance, salvation, and healing for another person. But if you tune your ears and say, "Father, You're here. What need is it that You want to meet?" Even saying, "I'm blessed to be a blessing, I'm in this place, who needs a blessing?" this is a level of confidence that comes from walking in the faith of God.

You can't do anything on your own, but when you tap into the faith *of* God, you can do everything! You can tune yourself to the heartbeat of Jesus, and He will do something through you, a willing vessel. And why is that? Because *He* is willing!

In all these Scriptures that we've been discussing, I believe that your faith is touching Jesus' faith, and your faith is being activated. In the conclusion, we will do a faith activation together so you can shift your faith and see miracles, healings, and the power of God activated in your life. Before that, though, we have one more chapter that will help you move into greater faith.

CHAPTER 15

THE HEAVENLY COURTROOM

W hat was written in the scrolls before the foundation of the world about each and every person on earth is important to God. In this chapter, you will be positioned to be set free to step into what God has for you. You are more than victorious in Christ. You can come to the throne of grace in your time of need to receive mercy, forgiveness, and healing, and to receive the acceptance that only God can give.

In November 2017, God began to tell me He was going to send me away January 11-13, 2018, to the Elijah List conference in Portland, Oregon. Supernaturally, He made a way financially for me to go and also gave me the time off from ministering at my church home. I didn't know why I was going to the conference exactly, but I knew I had to go and He had made provision for it. I did not even realize why He had sent me until I was there for twenty-four hours and I was listening to the second message that Apostle Robert Henderson brought forth on the Courts of Heaven.

I understood the Courts of Heaven and have since read Robert's book on this subject titled *Operating in the Courts of Heaven: Granting God the Legal Right to Fulfill His Passion and Answer Our Prayers*.[1] I had heard of the apostolic anointing on Robert's life, and the words that God had given him in the past about the courtrooms of Heaven, and so I figured, *Well, I already know pretty much what he's going to say, but I can't wait to hear the new spin on it because every year that you walk out a truth, God gives a greater revelation of that truth.*

After he started speaking for a couple moments, I felt that God was doing something huge in this room of people. I asked, *Lord, what's happening here? There's an impartation that is coming from this conference through what this man is saying.* And again, he was ministering primarily what he had already written in his book.

I felt so strongly that something different was taking place. Well, near the end of his presentation, he asked everybody to stand up, and he began to impart heavily from Heaven an anointing for the people who were at that place and those connected to the people in that place, that their destinies would come to pass that year. He said if there were hindrances or things that were holding back destiny, they would be broken in that moment. He framed the declaration like this: In past years, or even in the current year for you, for me, for all of us, as we stepped into destiny the past year, there may still be things hindering our destiny that we need to confess and get rid of in order to be able to fully step into the new year.

REPENTANCE IS A GIFT

You should constantly be in a state of repentance as a Christian. Repentance is a gift from God. If you are a believer, you have the Holy Spirit inside you, so God will be convicting you on a recurring basis. That's who He is. He does that because He wants us to stay aware of who He is and what He's done for us on the Cross already. It's not to give us a guilt complex. It's not to condemn us. It's to quicken us into continual and delightful fellowship with Him. It's to position us so we understand the access we have to Heaven, and where that access may be hindered. We have all things through the blood of Christ. We have been given all things. So, there is nothing that can legitimately block us from receiving all that God has for us. There is nothing that can stand in the way of our destiny if we are in a constant state of repentance.

PRAYER OF AGREEMENT

Apostle Robert Henderson took this group, in the Spirit, to a place of agreement in the heavenly courtroom that eliminated what happened in the previous year that held us back from having access to Heaven. In other words, we could now share with the people we minister to that those who are faithful to confess and repent, the hindrances attached to their destinies will be removed.

This is why this word is so powerful—we have an accuser, satan, and he goes before the throne of God to accuse us of how we live, that we may not be in line with the Word of God. He goes before the throne all the time to accuse us—but who does he find waiting there? Jesus our Advocate saying, "By My blood that I shed on the Cross, these people are set free. They are not to be condemned. They are not to suffer from guilt and condemnation. They will have everlasting life. They will fulfill the plan and purpose I have for them!"

We have Jesus as our Advocate who is ready and willing to consistently stand in our defense. The enemy comes and says, "But do you know what just happened? Do you know what that person just did?!"

Even still, the Bible says, *"...But if anybody does sin, we have an advocate with the Father—Jesus Christ, the Righteous One. He is the atoning sacrifice for our sins, and not only for ours but also for the sins of the whole world"* (1 John 2:1-2).

The most powerful thing about this conference for me personally was that I confessed, repented, and was released from all accusations that had been brought against me by satan. I actually felt like my destiny could be jump-started again and any accusations were now broken. We still need to repent and confess every day. Human flesh does wrong sometimes whether we know it or we don't know it. But there are choices we make in life that prevent the fullness of our destinies from occurring.

Listen, you're going to Heaven if you are born again and have confessed your sin and received Jesus Christ as your Lord and Savior. What I am talking about here is not salvation-focused. Unless you're reading this book today and you do not know Jesus as your Lord and Savior, you are on your way to Heaven. This message is not just for the person who needs to be born again. This message is for those who are born again, saved by grace. God has written in the scrolls of Heaven, even before the foundations of the world were laid, every day of what our lives are ordained to be. We know that.

Think about what this verse in Psalm 139 says about that, *"Your eyes saw my unformed body; all the days ordained for me were written in your book before one of them came to be"* (Ps. 139:16). Every day of your life was ordained even before you were born. So because of this, God wrote somewhere in the scrolls of Heaven about you and what His destiny and His plan was for you.

Now the accuser of the believers cannot come before the Father and condemn us to hell if we are saved, but what he can do is say,

"They will not fulfill their destiny on the planet because they've been engaging in X, Y, and Z sins." Revelation 12:10 says:

> *Then I heard a loud voice in heaven say: "Now have come the salvation and the power and the kingdom of our God, and the authority of his Messiah. For the accuser of our brothers and sisters, who accuses them before our God day and night, has been hurled down."*

Your salvation is secure, but what's not secure is whether or not you reach the fulfillment of your destiny and the plans and purposes that God has for you. That takes a whole lot more than us saying, "I believe in Jesus as my Lord and Savior." It means turning your whole life over to God and being committed to stay on the plan, path, and purpose that God has, and being determined that you're going to set aside everything in your life that would bring hindrance to that.

Just because we have delays in our destinies doesn't mean our destiny won't take place. It is true that there is spiritual warfare and demonic forces that come against us to stop our destiny, and we may have a part in that depending on whether or not our flesh is active in certain unrighteous activities. The accuser of the believers can go before the Lord and say, "Well, You should know what she does over here," or "I want to tell you what he does over there." And God will say "You know what, you're right. That's the truth. But when they confess and repent, I can set their course straight again."

Let me return to the story about the conference where Robert Henderson was speaking. He asked the conference attendees to go into prayer together corporately, but then also imparted to us the faith to go into the courtroom of Heaven to position others to do the same thing. It was an impartation for us to be free but also for us to free others. God began to speak to me, and I wept. I was very touched in my heart and prayed, "My God, this is just so amazing what's happening here." I began to feel in my spirit that God was erasing every poor decision that I made in the prior year. Any area that my free will went, God was now erasing on the Cross of Jesus Christ. I was being cleansed.

You can love God and still make poor decisions. One of the gifts that God gave us is our free will. I know sometimes it feels like a curse, but it's a gift. I remember when I first got saved, I said, "Lord, please just take the free will from me please. I want You to take it from me because You do not want to leave me with this. I will make the wrong choices." I was so unsure of myself. But as I grew with God, I began to like the fact I have free will because then I can love Him and follow Him and feel incredibly satisfied in making the right choices that He's calling me to make—knowing that I'm doing it together in unity with Him. This can be your free-will experience as well.

Now back to the story, I began to feel that God was wiping away all of my sins and poor decisions of that year and anything that was hindering my personal destiny. This realization was so overwhelmingly powerful for me. Some people were weeping and some were not. Everybody is on their own journey with God. But He clearly sent me there to get my cleansing. I was sent there because of what the enemy had accused me of before the Father.

The same is true for you. The enemy has gone before the Father and made accusations about you. He knows about the open doors in your life leading to unrighteousness, with some faults you may not have even been aware of; but nonetheless they are enough that the enemy had the power to stop some of your destiny from being fulfilled and delayed simply because he had the goods. He knew where you had been and what you had been thinking and doing that were against God, and you didn't even know it.

Again, I'm not talking about salvation. No, this is about destiny. It's about the fact that God has a plan for you, and a purpose; there's a reason why God has you here on earth to fulfill your purpose and to live the abundant life. If you have unfulfilled dreams, you have to ask the questions: What is causing the delay? Is this delay seasonal? Is it just not my time yet? Or is there delay because the enemy's got something on me?

Maybe you're not aware of what it is, and God needs to make you aware. Maybe you are aware of what it is, and it's time to put it away. It's time to put it under your feet. It's time to come clean.

In another service, God said to me, "Tonight I'm going to clean the slate for those who have felt delay in reaching their destiny. Those who have felt as though they have a plan and purpose but they can't quite get there. Or if they're not quite stepping into the place I have for them." When I left the Elijah List conference and the Courts of Heaven impartation, I arrived home clean. I returned to Freedom Destiny Church and God set the people free there when I shared my testimony, and then I walked them through the same impartation Robert Henderson passed on to us at the Elijah List conference.

BREAKING THE COMMANDMENTS

In the following passage in Exodus, the Word says:

> *Moses chiseled out two stone tablets like the first ones and went up Mount Sinai early in the morning, as the Lord had commanded him; and he carried the two stone tablets*

in his hands. Then the Lord came down in the cloud and stood there with him and proclaimed his name, the Lord. And he passed in front of Moses, proclaiming, "The Lord, the Lord, the compassionate and gracious God, slow to anger, abounding in love and faithfulness, maintaining love to thousands, and forgiving wickedness, rebellion and sin. Yet he does not leave the guilty unpunished; he punishes the children and their children for the sin of the parents to the third and fourth generation." Moses bowed to the ground at once and worshiped. "Lord," he said, "if I have found favor in your eyes, then let the Lord go with us. Although this is a stiff-necked people, forgive our wickedness and our sin, and take us as your inheritance." Then the Lord said: "I am making a covenant with you. Before all your people I will do wonders never before done in any nation in all the world. The people you live among will see how awesome is the work that I, the Lord, will do for you" (Exodus 34:4-10).

In this passage, God is speaking about the fact that laws were violated. In the violation of the laws, whether by sin, transgression, or iniquity, there was a breach. Let me define what these three breaches are:

1. *Sin* means a specific offense, meaning there's a specific breaking of a commandment.

2. A *transgression* is a revolt or a rebellion such as a repeated sin that is not stopped. In other words, you just keep doing it over and over again.

3. An *iniquity* is the Hebrew word *avon*, which means perversity, punishment of sin, and is connected to a

deeper Hebrew word *avan,* which means crook, or wickedly wrong. It is more about a character issue or deep root in your heart. It is a type of attitudinal bent from our families; it refers to a generational iniquity. Generational iniquity could also be generational curses, which are not something that you brought upon yourself but something that the generations before you brought upon you today.

Sin, iniquity, and transgression all went on the Cross of Jesus Christ; and as He was nailed to the Cross, you were also nailed with Him on the Cross. When He was buried, you were buried with Him; and when He was resurrected, you were resurrected with sin, transgression, and iniquity defeated. Paul tells us this, *"We were therefore buried with him through baptism into death in order that, just as Christ was raised from the dead through the glory of the Father, we too may live a new life"* (Rom. 6:4).

The Book of Exodus was written long before the Lord Jesus came to walk the earth and die for our sins, transgressions, and iniquity. The Word says the transgressions and the iniquity of the ancestors are placed upon the children and the children's children from generation to generation (Exod. 34:7). When we talk about cleaning a slate for a person, we are also talking about standing in the gap for generational iniquity or curses that are part of the family bloodline that came even before we were born. Do you know the enemy still goes before the Father on behalf of that iniquity? This is what satan can use to accuse us. There's nothing that can stop your destiny apart from you not repenting in the areas that God is calling you to repent of or to ask for the forgiveness of generations before you as Daniel did in the Book of Daniel 9:3-19.

Our God cleans up your soul over time. You can't possibly repent of everything that needs to be repented of in one sitting. Throughout your life, you learn the things about which God wants to deal with you. When the Holy Spirit is present, after you get saved, He will clean up your act, just because you know Him. You don't have to give people the law after they're saved because God takes care of that. If His Holy Spirit is inside them, people are going to start dropping stuff they don't want to be part of anymore, and they don't even know why. It's because they've become the temple of the Holy Spirit.

Some people say, "Oh, you know we can't let *that* person in the Church. Do you know what they are doing?!" What? We can't be afraid of what someone is doing. We can't be afraid of sin. No, invite people to come and connect with the Lord—give them a front-row seat. And when the anointing of God hits them, they'll be on their knees or laid out. Don't worry about cleaning people up, because you can't do it. Only God can do it.

When we talk about scratching a bad year in our life or repenting of sins, transgression, iniquity, whatever is preventing us from stepping into destiny, we must see it from the standpoint that God will bring up only so much for now, and next year we'll have to deal with something else.

DESTINY BOUND

God wants to take care of us now! He wants to pardon our iniquities, our sins, or our transgressions; in other words, He wants us to come to that place of confession and repentance and allow Him to take care of what's standing in the way of our destiny. The blood of Jesus takes care of all of this for you today. God says in Exodus:

I am making a covenant with you. Before all your people I will do wonders never before done in any nation in all the world. The people you live among will see how awesome is the work that I, the Lord, will do for you (Exodus 34:10).

God is saying to you right now, when you're faithful to come before the Lord and confess and repent and open your heart to Him, He's going to do amazing, miraculous, and beautiful things as a result of your obedience. It means that there's not only destiny before you, there's the greatest of all—a deep and abiding relationship with Him because that's where our destiny begins.

You see, the destiny that He wrote in the scrolls about your life involves Him. Destiny alone means nothing unless He's in it with you. This is why free will is a blessing. Free will connected to Him brings about a destiny where you get to experience and encounter God while He brings you to the fulfillment of all that He created you for. So yes, free will is a gift, because it causes us to have to make the conscious choice and decide to ask God to clean up these areas in our lives.

It also means we have a free will to be stubborn and rebellious and stiff-necked, and may even think, *Hmm, I don't need to repent.* You have a free will to do that too. But if you do that, I'm here to tell you, next year is *not* going to look much better than last year. You'll figure it out halfway through the year, but you could figure it out here, now, at the end of this book and have it all taken care of sooner than later.

After I received that impartation at the Elijah List conference, and I realized the impartation didn't come until after I asked God to clean my slate, I said, "God, You have to clean my slate. There are some things that I can't take into the new year. I don't want to mess up my destiny. I don't want to go in any wrong direction. I want to stay on the clear path, God. And Lord, I ask for Your forgiveness, that You would keep me on the right path, and that I would make the right choices and decisions. I really want that God, because I really want whatever it is that You've written in the scrolls of Heaven about me."

Do you know that the Word tells us that there's a scroll written in Heaven about Jesus? He actually says that specifically in Hebrews:

> *Therefore, when Christ came into the world, he said: "Sacrifice and offering you did not desire, but a body you prepared for me; with burnt offerings and sin offerings you were not pleased. Then I said, 'Here I am—it is written about me in the scroll—I have come to do your will, my God'"* (Hebrews 10:5-7).

There's a scroll in Heaven written about you too. The will of God is on it. If you made decisions over the past year that took you off His path, then in this last chapter, through a prayer of repentance, God will put you back on the right path simply because you decided to confess, "You know what, I got off Your path, Lord. Please show me the way back."

All of us make mistakes! No one is perfect. If you have raised children, you know they go off the path all the time, and you try not to say too much because you want them to make the right decision to get back on track on their own. Our heavenly Father sees us the same way.

The accuser of the believers, satan, is always ready to say, "Hey God, did You see that? Did You see what that kid just did? See, Your kid is not willing to give that up." But God says, "Listen, I'm going to give My children another chance. I give them unlimited chances to make it right because I have a destiny written for them in the scrolls."

PRAYER OF RELEASE INTO DESTINY

I'm excited to walk you through a prayer right now. In this prayer, you are not only going to repent for yourself, but you're going to repent for your family. I will also share some things I see in the spirit realm in this prayer and prophesy. Just repeat the following prayer and watch God release you into your destiny!

Lord, I'm coming forward with a heart to want to take care of what is standing in the way of Your perfect will, plan, and destiny for my life. God, I thank You right now for Your Holy Spirit presence coming into this place. Lord Jesus, begin to stir in my heart.

Lord, I thank You, Father, that brokenness in me and broken relationships will be mended. Where husbands and wives have been pitted against each other. You will mend this, Father. Where confession needs to be done on both sides, where they need to get on with the plan that You have for them as a couple and as a family, lead us in this. Lord, we pray for the children who have been disobedient. If they have ignored the requests of their parents for the good that You've called them to, God, we ask for repentance for the children, Father.

Father, we repent of anger and of harsh words that have been said one to another in our families. Where we chose not to speak life. Where we chose to speak death. Lord, bring Your healing presence into this house, God. In such a way, Father, that You wipe the slate clean. Lord, we repent of husbands and wives who have purposely discon-nected from one another. May the one flesh be reunited. Lord, we repent of where we were not a good neighbor to another person. Or we were not neighborly to them. Or we did not love on others the way that we should.

Lord, I repent of anytime we were afraid to use the spir-itual gifts that You gave us. These gifts were part of Your destiny plan, but we held on to our gifts because we wanted to steward them for ourselves, and not for the Kingdom of God. Father, forgive us.

Lord, we repent as the Ecclesia, the Church, for we may have missed a need in the community. Where we put resources or a lack of that in front of a call or something that You have told us to do. We repent of where and when we were not holy in any respect. Holy with our bodies, where we put our bodies in a place or position where we were not among holiness and we engaged in unholy activi-ties, we repent, Father.

I see in the spirit realm people who have gone to places that are unholy in order to help others who needed to be helped; but while they were there, they found they weren't strong enough to be there by themselves and fell prey to what was around them.

We repent where we have not put You first, Father, but where You were last. You were last in our thoughts; You were last in our hearts. The things of the world were first. We repent of that, Father. Lord, there's so many things that are being laid at this altar right now with You. Each one of them were choices and decisions that we made, whether we were lured away by the enemy to do it, whether we wanted to do it, or whether we didn't want to do it. Whether it was generational iniquity or curses, transgressions, or sin.

You have heard our hearts, God, as we come before You. I see the hearts of people crying out as the prayers are going up. Each and every person's prayers going up, going up, going up, going up to the throne of God.

Oh, we thank You, Father, that as the prayers go up, Lord Jesus, the confession goes up. We thank You, Father, that You're hearing, that You're receiving. We thank You that the enemy is weakening, God. When he comes before the throne, he's getting weaker, Father, because our prayers and confessions are getting stronger.

Lord, we thank You that the ground cries out. Just as the blood of Abel cried out, God. Murder, adultery, fornication, sexual sin, it all rises to You, Father. The enemy, he can't bring it forth because a confession positions Jesus to be our Advocate. A confession positions Jesus to say, "Father, look at My blood, for they are forgiven." I thank You, Father, that You gave us Jesus to stand in the gap, to mend our relationship with You, to unite us with You in such a way that our destinies will come to pass. That no matter what the enemy came to stand before You with, the blood of Jesus cries out boldly, "They are forgiven. They are not guilty. They are not condemned." And healing and cleanliness and purity and salvation and grace, all of these are falling from Heaven upon each and every person who reads this book.

I see the destinies of people coming to pass. I see them running a race. They're not tiring. They're not getting weary. They're not stopping because there's no weight or encumbrance keeping them from their destiny. We'll keep on praying, because our prayers are rising.

Lord, dig deep. Holy Spirit, dig deep. Thank You, Jesus. I thank You, Father, that as we become clean, we can become advocates for others. Come to the throne of grace to receive mercy. Oh, hallelujah! I see that where there's been lies, where there's been manipulation, where there's been control, where there's been fear, it's dissipating. Where we told lies because we were afraid or confused, God, You're wiping it away. You're wiping it away right now. Lord, make us truthtellers. Just as You are the King of truth, may we be truthtellers.

I see weakness and imperfection that God does not hold against you, but you hold against yourself. May you raise up and be more confident. Weakness and imperfection cannot keep you from your destiny, but you have to choose to be confident. Weakness and imperfection feel a lot like guilt and condemnation. It feels like we're not able to accomplish what God has before us. But the Lord says rise above. You have every reason to rise above. Every reason. You have the Holy Spirit inside you. He's perfect. He's without weakness. He is victorious. You rest in Him.

I see you getting lighter and wearing less burdens. Lord, we cry out to You for healing. God, come and bring a deep healing as we confess and repent. Lord, let the glory cloud descend on this reader who is praying now. Let us feel the glory.

Someone has a new voice rising—someone You want to speak through. Windows of Heaven. Lord, You're opening the windows of Heaven. Thank You, Lord Jesus.

PRAYERS TO RELEASE OTHERS

As your prayer and confession have gone up to Heaven and your slate is wiped clean, now we are going to pray that you realize you are forgiven and are willing to walk in the authority from Heaven to help walk others into this place of freedom. That you would feel the authority to go into the courtroom of Heaven and cast your case on behalf of family members and friends whose destinies are delayed in this moment.

You will be able to go in to the courtroom of Heaven and say, "I was one who needed to confess and repent, and I did and I received. So now I come on behalf of others and ask the Father, that You would help them walk through that process as well, and that You would help me help them walk through that process, Lord, that they may open the door to the throne of grace. That they might feel You drawing them to that place of confession and repentance. That place of getting their destiny right this year."

Father, I praise You and I thank You right now that it was imparted to me at the conference, Lord, to be one who helps walk others through the process of releasing Heaven. That people You put in my path would be ones who would help others walk through that process as well. Give them confidence to go into the throne room, into the courtroom of Heaven, and to plead their case on behalf of others and say, "Lord, help them. Help them come to the place of confession and repentance so they may have their destiny reignited."

You can't go to a place, or take anybody to a place that you haven't already been. It's not possible. God doesn't work it out that way. See, you have to go there first so that you can help other people get from here to there. So, since you've been willing to walk to the courtroom of Heaven and cast confession and repentance, to be acquitted, forgiven, and justified by the blood of Jesus, now you have the authority to walk others to that place, because you were willing to go there yourself.

> *Father, I praise You and I thank You that this impartation is so people will stand up and do what they've been called to do, which is to go into the courtroom on behalf of others who cannot go themselves, and stand and plead their case. In that courtroom, You will listen because they have come before you and have been forgiven. They're standing in the blood of Jesus, which is the only reason I can stand here. It's the only reason anyone stands before Your throne— because of the blood of Jesus.*

But we need people to walk with us. That's what paracletes do, that's what servants do. That's what the servants of God do, they walk others into that place. You've been given authority under Heaven and earth to walk people into the throne room of Heaven, at any time, and come before the King, and profess what He has done on the Cross for you. Then the people you take there will be set free. The strongholds will be broken!

I see you doing this with your family members. I see you going into neighborhoods. I see you going all over and saying to others,

"What you can't do for yourself, I'm going to do for you now. I'm going to walk you into God's presence and He is going to release Heaven over you." And you're going to pray prayers for people that will help take them into the throne room of Heaven where they can confess and repent and be forgiven and be set free.

> *Lord, we praise You and we thank You because You truly are the Victor. You truly have done it all for us. You're empowering us to walk in the way that You have already walked, and to carry out what You have already done for us, God. We thank You, Lord, that this is part of our destiny, to be mouthpieces and voices and members of Your body who help care for others who can't care for themselves; and in doing so, carry out the gospel of the Kingdom of God.*

> *Lord, we thank You for the destiny You have for us this year and how we will grab hold of it and walk into the places that You've called us into. Father, we praise You and we thank You.*

> *Lord, together we agree that there have been areas in our lives, things that have happened that have stopped us from obtaining the fullness You have for us.*

Every believer has those areas individually, but we also have them as a Kingdom Church body. We may not fully know what is holding us back, we may only know partially. It's Heaven's job, the Holy Spirit's job, to reveal it to us. We may spiritually sense something's not right but can't quite put our finger on it. By confession and repentance, we make the foundation firm enough for God to begin to catapult us, launch us into our destiny.

Trust God as He catapults you into your destiny where you will be a Kingdom expander who creates supernatural environments for heavenly encounters. You have been made clean and whole by the blood of Jesus; you triumphed over the enemy by the blood of the Lamb and by the word of your testimony (Rev. 12:11). Remember, you are a citizen of Heaven first, and you have the power to release Heaven every day because of what Jesus did for you!

ENDNOTE

1. For more information on how to pray specifically for your needs as God reveals, I highly recommend Apostle Robert Henderson's book, *Operating in the Courts of Heaven: Granting God the Legal Right to Fulfill His Passion and Answer Our Prayers* (Shippensburg, PA: Destiny Image Publishers, 2016). This book gives you specifics on how to access the courts of Heaven in all cases and the theology behind it. This prayer was Holy Spirit-prompted for this book but is not exhaustive like the one in Apostle Henderson's book.

CONCLUSION

Heavenly encounters are keys to changing supernatural environments and God wants to use you as a heavenly portal, a glory portal, for Him to do His work on this planet. I hope that while you read these chapters your faith was activated and you actually believe God wants to use you, just as you are.

Jesus says, *"You are already clean because of the word I have spoken to you"* (John 15:3). He is now expecting you to go:

> *Then Jesus came to them and said, "All authority in heaven and on earth has been given to me. Therefore go and make disciples of all nations, baptizing them in the name of the Father and of the Son and of the Holy Spirit, and teaching them to obey everything I have commanded you. And surely I am with you always, to the very end of the age"* (Matthew 28:18-20).

You are a disciple with a mandate to release Heaven to earth so that people can walk in the authority of Heaven and participate with God to bring salvation, healing, and deliverance to the earthly realm. You need the faith of God, or God kind of faith, for this journey.

FAITH ACTIVATION PRAYER

As we conclude this book, I want to pray an activation prayer that will impart to you so you can go forth and begin to walk in the faith of God for miracles and healings. God wants you on the front lines of His army with the angelic hosts bringing good news to the world. This is where you must walk in the confidence of knowing your identity in Christ and all He has done for you in your death, burial, and resurrection in Him. You are a new creature and you have the power. Let us pray:

> *Lord, I thank You now for activating the faith of the person reading this prayer right now. That they will be overcome with Your Spirit power and develop such a deep and intimate relationship with You that they are forever changed inside and begin to see You as the only One willing and able to heal and deliver. That this person's faith may be activated to release Heaven in every circumstance in their life as they keep a deep and abiding relationship connection with You and focus on You.*
>
> *I pray, Lord, that You teach this reader the secrets of the Kingdom of Heaven on earth and that open-Heaven encounters become a daily occurrence as they open their seer eyes to watch for You and join You. That they learn to touch and agree with You in a moment and release Heaven. That they learn to walk in power and confidence,*

and that doubt and fear is removed now. That they learn to participate with the angelic host to bring about healing and miracles in their life and the lives of others.

I thank You, God, that You will encourage this reader to step out right after this book is closed and begin to listen more clearly to Your instructions and follow them. I thank You, heavenly Father, that You will show up and do what You need to do. We pray for words of knowledge and wisdom and for the prophetic to begin to flow in this friend's life now. I pray they walk in healing and miracles, and that they will not be hindered by anything, but simply respond to Your loving Spirit, ready to bless one another.

I thank You, Jesus, that this dear reader is ready to go now and release Heaven to earth in his or her soul, home, workplace, church, all environments to which You call them. You are worthy, Lord, and we give You all the praise and thanksgiving. We thank You, Father, for activating the spiritual gifts in this person's life and that there is right now a feeling of change, in Jesus' name, amen.

Now you are ready to *go!*

I encourage you to email me and let me know how God is using you in a mighty way. I would like to hear your testimony so I can share it. Heaven is a heartbeat away, and you are the one God is using to bring it here!

About the Author

Dr. Candice Smithyman is an apostolic and prophetic minister. She is the founder and executive pastor of Freedom Destiny Church and founder of Dream Mentors International, a biblical and transformational life-coaching school. She hosts the *Glory Road* TV show on Faith Networks and multiple internet outlets. Dr. Smithyman has authored many books and writes for online publications including *Elijah List, Charisma, Prophetic 365,* and *Spirit Fuel.*

Please send personal testimonies of how this book has impacted your life to:

Info@candicesmithyman.com

https://www.candicesmithyman.com

https://www.dreammentors.org

Instagram @candicesmithyman

Listen to Dr. Candice's *On the Glory Road* podcast on the Destiny Image Podcast Network